VALUE in HEALTH CARE

what is it & and how
do we create it?

VALUE in HEALTH CARE

what is it & and how do we create it?

Jonathan D. Hart, MD, MBA

valueinhealthcare.org

Book Cover and Interior Design by The Book Cover Whisperer: ProfessionalBookCoverDesign.com

Book Cover Illustration by Lin Hart

978-0-5788053-4-4 Hardcover
978-0-5787936-9-6 Paperback
978-0-5787937-0-2 eBook

Printed in the United States of America

FIRST EDITION

Dedicated to Thom Andrews, who devoted himself

to teaching us to see the worth of people

and the value of relationship.

CONTENTS

Acknowledgments

THANKS TO Denise Buckland, Carolyn Tinsley, Andy Tibbetts, Lynne Thorp, Paul Simeone, Robert Millette, and Emily Kiernan for showing me the principles of Population Health Management in action as Value-based Care and for helping me find words to describe these concepts.

Preface

———

AS CONSUMERS, WE WANT to gain the most value from any purchase we make. We perceive that value through a subconscious calculation we perform numerous times a day—what was the quality of the item or service compared to its cost multiplied by my experience? Businesses in almost all industries know this, and they strive to optimize our perceived value through price, quality, or service/experience. Segments of business that don't concern themselves with creating value seek to simply sell as much product or service they can until the consuming public grows wise or finds an alternative. Over the past century, healthcare in the United States has been this type of industry, oblivious to value creation. Thankfully, though, this is starting to change. The problem is that many purveyors of healthcare don't understand value or how to create it.

The two main paradigms within which most modern businesses function are volume and value. Volume is based solely on piecework. The more product or service produced and sold at the highest possible price, the more revenue for the company. These two parameters are the only consideration in volume—price and quantity. Value, on the other hand, relies on the proper balance of quality, cost, and experience. Many have limited value to simply a ratio of quality and cost, but I suggest that the experience of the customer (as well as for the "production" stakeholders) is a multiplier in this equation. Revenue is dependent on the organization's ability to create value and maintain its customers.

Most healthcare dollars today in the US are spent in what's known as fee for service, volume-based care. Moreover, it's not the consumer of the service—the patient—who typically pays for that service. The conventional pattern of US healthcare is episodic treatment of the patient for their current problem and then the generation of a claim to a separate entity who then pays the bill. This volume-based, disconnected process has led the US to have a dysfunctional health system. We Americans spend more money than any other nation on healthcare expenses, but we are barely in the Top Twenty in terms of health outcomes among our peer nations.

Given that our healthcare delivery system is based on volume, with no regard for quality outcomes or experience, it should not surprise anyone that we don't fare better against our peers in cost or outcomes. A movement has emerged within the healthcare industry over recent years promoting a shift toward value. The change from our current defective and incapable system based on fee for service and volume of services rendered rather than patient outcomes is seen as necessary to improve our quality of care and patient experience while maintaining appropriate costs—in other words, the creation of value. The US Centers for Medicare Administration has pointed to value creation as its goal in its "Triple Aim" statement of goals to improve the individual experience of care, improve the health of populations, and reduce the per capita costs of care for populations.

The primary objectives of healthcare should be to allow patients to feel cared for and to facilitate the optimization of their health and well-being.

A movement has emerged within the healthcare industry over recent years promoting a shift toward value.

The value model facilitates these through the proper alignment of incentives for the stakeholders—patients, providers, staff, facilities, insurers (including the government), suppliers, etc. In addition to the appropriate motivations for stakeholders, the creation of value, through the intentional improvement of experience, emphasizes how the human stakeholders—patients, providers, and staff—are valued as active individual participants in the process. A volume mindset, on the other hand, relegates these people to the level of commodities—cogs and widgets in the healthcare machine. This change in mindset can be transformative for US healthcare, as it encourages engagement, communication, and collaboration.

Considering patients as humans rather than diagnoses also means that, beyond looking solely at their medical conditions, their lives must be assessed in circumferential totality and addressed to optimize their health. We need to identify their social risks, behavioral risks, and mental health conditions as diligently and routinely as we currently assess physical vital signs in patients. Furthermore, we need to develop and implement effective means through which we can attend to these issues once identified.

Proper plans of care can best be developed when we know all that is affecting our patients. By grouping the patients' needs in analysis, we can also find patterns that lead us, as organizations, as an industry, and as a society, to develop systematic processes to carry out those plans more efficiently and effectively. Gathering, analyzing, and acting on data in this manner is the foundation of Population Health Management. The processes developed can be multiple and standard as we build out the necessary infrastructure to meet our patients' needs. Patient plans, however, are unique and individual, and use the developed processes in a combination directed toward the specific needs of that particular patient.

The attention to patients' needs in devising how healthcare is delivered does not necessarily need to negatively impact provider revenue, even though we're aiming to rein in costs. In healthcare, like most other industries, when system and process design are based on the best interests and outcomes of the consumers, revenue will follow. Focus on the true medical needs of the patient, on their appropriate navigation through our healthcare maze, and on the proper stewardship of healthcare coverage premium dollars will reduce the current waste and preserve revenue while allowing patients to optimize their health and well-being.

All of this points to creating value in healthcare through the applied concepts of Population Health Management–improving the health of a population one patient at a time through the collection, analysis, and application of data to meet the needs of a cohort through the vehicle of Value-based Care. At its core, Population Health Management is the process of stratifying patients by risk, assessing and documenting potential negative impactors on patient's well-being, building a plan of care for the individual patient based on best medical practices and the distinct needs of the patient, and then providing longitudinal support to patients, effectively and efficiently communicating the collaborative plan of care to all involved.

In the Hills of Appalachia

————

THE SERVICE ORGANIZATION FOR which I worked in the mid-1990s as a physician and medical director sits in a valley along the riverside and offers a K–12 school, social and medical services, and a thrift store that provides inexpensive shopping for clothing and home goods. Like most areas in the Appalachian region, life and construction followed the meandering whims of a river here, cutting an ever-deepening gorge between the opposing hills and mountains. Of course, the river flooded every spring, but the local people compensated by building stilted homes or simply moving up the slope when needed.

The main road, a two-lane highway, hugs the riverbank, flanked closely on the other side by a swath of trees, and the steep rise of the mountain. The opposite faces of the mountains crowded out the valley in most places, choosing the occasional wide bend in the river to spread out in a small oasis of flat land. Homes perched on the slopes of these hills, and many times a family shares its plot of land between numerous generations, whose structures clung higher and higher up the hillside as the family grew. Preserving family ties is important to these folks, and for many, staying close to home was a very high priority.

Most of the families in the area are descended from Scottish, Irish, and Welsh pioneers who settled in these highlands and then later worked the coal mines and logging camps that dominated the landscape for over a century. Yet toward the mid-to-late twentieth century, with the advent of technology, the demand for human hands in logging and mining waned, and the once busy mountain folks were engulfed by unemployment.

Some families, like Donna's (I am using pseudonyms for all patients), live off the main road, up one of the hollows, or as we called them, hollers. Donna lived in the hills of this Appalachian region of the United States in the mid-1990s, and I cared for her and her family. Even then, she was an elderly woman with diabetes, hypertension, and heart failure, which often accompanies these two chronic conditions over time. Her widowed daughter Betty cared for in her home with assistance from her disabled adult grandson Michael. This family had much in common with many others in that area in terms of where and how they lived, and how they had adapted to the changing world in an area that the rest of the country might easily have forgotten.

The pavement soon gave way to gravel and then narrowed to a one-way, tree branch-canopied, grass-centered path splattered with the sun's rays flickering through the thick mantle of leaves—unless, like Donna, you lived on the sunless north side of the hill. At times it would feel to me as if I were entering a land hidden from civilization—until a close shave with the UPS truck passing me going out of the holler as I was going in abruptly awakened me to the reality of the modern day.

In several ways, it felt as if the rest of the world had forgotten the people of this area, as it does most people living in impoverished areas. True, their jobs had been moved, their lifestyle disrupted, and their faith shaken. But they were still acutely aware of the world around them. Satellite dishes and the internet brought them the sights and sounds as well as the expectations of the world beyond the hills. The youth had moved on from Bluegrass to Hip-Hop. The independent spirit of their mountain ancestors remained, but the reality was that many residents depended greatly on the governmental programs (like Food Stamps and Medicaid) put in place to compensate for the extreme loss of jobs over the prior fifty years. Moonshine, while still available, was giving way to the first signs of the opioid crisis in the US. In this, Appalachia was actually ahead of the rest of the country. The government had built new and well-constructed main roads and public schools, but the people's faces often reflected the wear and tear, and angst, of a community that had repeatedly weathered adversity.

This was the backdrop to my years as a provider of medical services in Appalachia to people like Donna, Betty, and Michael— proud families with a history of hard work, people committed to each other and the river and hollers of their birth, people buoyed by their ever-present adaptability in the face of life's and society's constant floods.

I didn't know it at the time, but this would be my first exposure to what we now call Population Health Management and Value-based Care. Some of the patients my colleagues and I treated in the medical center were funded by fee-for-service government sources–Medicare and Medicaid–but many were subsidized through private funding from philanthropic donations. These patients were the ones who most needed applied Population Health concepts, though all, including Donna, would have benefited from them. From private donors, we oversaw a pot of money from which we had to provide care for all the folks whose expenses the state or federal governments weren't covering, and we needed to determine the best use of that money to bring the most benefit to that cohort.

I soon came to realize that the diagnostic and prescriptive

medical care represented only small portions of what the people in the area needed. In fact, on its own, the "medical care" we provided in the clinic, the lab, and through home health was not going to address or alleviate their medical problems and needs completely, let alone assist people in their journey toward improved health and well-being. The social

I didn't know it at the time, but this would be my first exposure to what we now call Population Health Management and Value-based Care.

pressures exerted on the residents of this region had a significantly more negative effect on their health than could be balanced by accurate diagnosis and best practice prescribing.

Donna's story is a great example. Though her care was covered by the federal government (Medicare), her social situation affected her health and well-being more negatively than did her chronic medical issues. She shared those chronic conditions with many others in the region, given the endemic nature of diabetes and hypertension, likely from a combination of genetic and social factors. The new roads provided little consolation to her family, as they struggled to find reliable transportation. The unemployment likewise endemic to the area made an adequate income source a challenge for them, as well.

The dietary staples in this household were fried baloney on

white bread, washed down with a sugary, highly caffeinated soda claiming the dewy attributes of the mountains. The closest food sources existed in some convenience stores scattered through the valleys, stores that also sold fuel. The food stocked in these mini-marts was highly processed to ensure a stable shelf-life. (I was not aware of the term "food desert" at this time in my career, but this area certainly would have qualified as one.) Getting other healthier groceries was difficult because the closest true grocery store was thirty-five miles through the mountains. That trip was an inconvenience for me and my family, but almost inconceivable for Donna's. While Donna's husband was still alive, they had had a garden in the summer, but any remnants of that were long gone, especially after his death and after a logging accident claimed the life of her son-in-law.

Tobacco use in this area helped bolster the state's claim to one of the highest rates of smoking in the nation. Donna didn't smoke due to her religious upbringing and beliefs, but her two home companions did. They kept the windows open in the summer, allowing a flow of air through the house rolling up the holler from the river valley below, and this helped compensate for the stale tobacco residue embedded in the walls as well as the slightly musty smell resulting from their north-facing, sun-impoverished homestead.

Donna's father had built the house around the beginning of the twentieth century with some renovations over the years. Wood-framed and low slung, it represented a typical mountain home in the region built in that era. The lack of the sun's touch to their side of the mountain made the home a bit dark, but it was welcoming nonetheless. A workcamp group from the mission had put on a new roof a couple of years back and rebuilt the porch a few years before that. The family kept the home clean, but the age of the house made it susceptible to the occasional pest problem—mostly mice and snakes. Indoor plumbing had been installed a couple of decades prior to my visits, but Donna still preferred to use the outdoor privy which, unfortunately, was located at the back of the house, slightly uphill from their stilted, mountainside home. The water that came from their taps was suitable for bathing and cooking, but run-off from the local mines meant they needed a different water source for drinking.

The primary income sources for this family were Donna's Social Security check and Michael's Social Security Disability check for his incapacitating depression. Since they couldn't afford reliable transportation on their own (and public transit was non-existent), the mission's pharmacy delivered Donna's medications. I shared the responsibility of home medical visits with the mission's home health service.

Meanwhile, the mission worried about how it could keep its doors open. How could they afford to minister to the folks in this area? It was painfully clear that we at the mission were no more than a band-aid on the gaping wound of social disparity. The local people needed jobs. They needed safe and affordable housing. They needed reliable transportation. And they needed care for all the chronic medical conditions exacerbated by their circumstances. Gathering enough resources to address all the needs, regardless of how many donations and pledges we obtained, was a monumental and perpetually looming task. Bringing in short term mission groups from around the US to repair roofs and update homes provided a revenue source for the mission and a stopgap for some problems, but in reality, such programs seemed only to take away the possibility for local labor and paying jobs.

In retrospect, to be most effective, we needed to assess the community's needs plus the needs of its individuals objectively and to build programs to address those needs. However, as a paper-based medical center in the late 1990s, our data lake was extremely shallow and difficult to navigate. Because of this lack of an accessible objective data source full of actionable insights, we functioned more on an anecdotal basis than on data-driven insights. Almost everyone in the area was under negative pressure from the social risks of food, housing, and employment insecurity plus endemic medical issues. So in addition to data on medical and social conditions, we needed a way to stratify these patients based on all their risks in order to start chipping away at the obstacles blocking the path to their optimum health and well-being.

How do you meet people where they are and address their needs without the ability to stratify patients based on risk? How do you develop meaningful, impactful plans followed up by appropriate support? The answers to these questions, I would discover later, are in the principles of Population Health Management and Value-based Care. The intent of this book is to explore changes we can make in our current healthcare delivery systems, through Population Health management and Value-based Care, in order to help families like Donna's and many others across the US landscape.

In addition to data on medical and social conditions, we needed a way to stratify these patients based on all their risks in order to start chipping away at the obstacles blocking the path to their optimum health and well-being.

On a basic level, we had engaged in the rudimentary principles of Population Health without realizing it. In order to spend the money raised from donations in the best possible way, we had to discern who most needed what services and focus efforts to those ends. More out of necessity than intentionality, we were exploring and assessing the patients' entire circumstances, and in doing so, uncovering social, cultural, and psychologic stumbling blocks impeding their medical progress to improved health and well-being. Based on these findings, anecdotal though they were, we employed and engineered ways to meet and support the patients where they were, give appropriate guidance within their cultural context, as well as push on the fringes of what some in the area would have considered the accepted norms. Unfortunately, we had to try to do this without the powerful tool of deep data pools that might provide us with actionable insights and predictive analytics. In this cumbersome process, how much value, if any, were we creating? Were we truly showing our patients (and staff) their value as humans, or were they just less effective cogs in a poorly-funded, tattered machine?

I saw people like Donna over and over again, people with chronic medical conditions as well as the complicating factors of poor housing, the lack of a good fresh food source, and inadequate reliable transportation. How many? I don't know. And that was the problem. We didn't track these findings of social risks–or even the incidence of chronic diseases–much less dig into for them and be able to glean actionable insights. We merely reacted in the moment.

How much more effective would we have been if we had actively assessed and addressed not only the chronic medical conditions endemic to the area but also the rampant social and mental health risks plaguing our patients? What if we'd had the computing power then that we now have to track, analyze, and act on needs and trends within a population? What if we had applied the current concepts of Population Health Management and created value in health care for these people?

It's tempting to think of the plight of these patients in Appalachia as unique to the region or time period. In fact, the prevalence of these and other social risks combined with chronic medical conditions exerting a negative impact on people's health and well-being is diffuse and growing today. No region or neighborhood is immune from the diagnoses or the social risks that exacerbate them. Without recognizing the conditions at play, building plans to address, mitigate or alleviate those conditions, and then supporting patients through their healthcare journeys, the story of my patient in the mountains will continue to be a

How much more effective would we have been if we had actively assessed and addressed not only the chronic medical conditions endemic to the area, but also the rampant social and mental health risks plaguing our patients?

familiar one throughout the US.

With this book, I hope to highlight how and why the concepts of Population Health Management through the applied vehicle of Value-based Care are essential to improve health and well-being, allowing patients to feel cared for, and actually create value in healthcare, an industry stuck in a volume-based paradigm.

Introduction to the Concepts

———

POPULATION HEALTH IS A concept that's been around since at least the 1990s. Though often seen as a lofty or academic concept, its true application to everyday function and care in the health industry has come to the forefront since the passage of the Affordable Care Act in 2010. There are still many organizations that only dabble in Population Health, putting it in a jar on the shelf, then taking it down now and again to show what they do in Pop Health. Others aren't completely clear on what Population Health Management or improvement is really about, so they slog through their days stuck in and committed to a world of decreasing payment for providing rescue services to their patients.

So what is Population Health and what is Population Health Management?

I officially started learning about Population Health and its ties to creating value in healthcare in 2009. That's the year I hung up my stethoscope to sit behind a desk for an insurance and utilization/care management company. Though we dealt with patients, providers, and facilities around the world, our main scope of domestic business in the US was providing utilization management (insurance authorizations for tests, medication or treatments prior to their initiation) and case management, disease management, and wellness services to small and mid-sized companies that self-funded their employee health plans.

I had spent the nineteen years prior to 2009 in clinical practice as a rural family medicine doc, an emergency physician, and a hospitalist, caring for patients and their families while managing physicians, working with and for hospital administrators, and dealing with insurance companies as a provider. I knew how to deliver high-quality care to my patients, but I'm not convinced I understood how to create value for them in their healthcare journeys. I wasn't contemplating cost. I didn't keep deep data files on my patients and evaluate them individually and as a group to see how well or not chronic conditions were being managed, nor did I screen patients for social risks that might impede their medical treatment.

I knew how to offer appropriate diagnosis and how to prescribe, and I've been told I delivered a great experience for my patients through an engaging bedside manner and a relentless dismantling of the barriers to the care they needed. However, I limited my practice scope to the medical ailments of my patients, only asking about social, psychological, and emotional impacts on their lives when it was painfully obvious that something non-medical was influencing their course. Also, we had no clue in our practice how many of our (for example) diabetic or hypertensive patients were actually taking their medicine, let alone were well-controlled. We sent out reminders for Pap smears and mammograms but couldn't have told you how many patients followed through with getting them. Nor could I have told you how many of my patients lived in a food desert because at that time I had no idea what a food desert was.

The closest I came to addressing the creation of value through appropriate cost was when some families told me they were struggling to make ends meet, and I would either undercharge them or not bill them at all. Today, I would handle this completely differently, but at the time, this was the only arrow I had in my quiver for this problem. The administrator of the hospital that owned our practice was not happy with me and insisted, "If these people don't have the money to pay for an office visit, then you can't see them!"

My response was to leave that practice and go work for a medical mission in Appalachia. In that setting, we simply assumed no one had resources, and we acted accordingly. It was there that we built a program to pool the money from churches' donations to cover the costs of our patients' care since many couldn't afford a fee-for-service model, even on our sliding scale. Too bad we lacked the tools and technology to track and analyze the various risks and needs of our patients in order to focus our efforts for the most positive impact. We don't have a similar excuse today, as our computing and data colleagues have brought us numerous innovations and platforms through which to gain a better view of what's happening in the lives of the patients we serve.

Back to my new career starting in 2009: self-funded employer healthcare plans helped me cut my teeth on Population Health principles and the creation of value in healthcare. Organizations that understood the concepts were concerned about optimizing their employees' health and well-being while controlling their health plans' costs. In other words, they were concerned with the creation of value.

During this same time, from the international perspective, our company delved deeper and deeper into the world of medical travel, sending patients all over the US and the world to get high quality care at a better price. As I visited some of these international destinations for healthcare, I saw in them a commitment to distinguish themselves from other potential providers through a concierge approach to patients and families—meaning that they built services, systems, and processes around the needs of the patients and their family members rather than for the convenience of staff and providers. This intentional effort facilitated a sense of being cared for in the patients and their loved ones, not only adding value to the experience but improving patient engagement and outcomes.

After six years, I left the payer side of healthcare to rejoin my colleagues on the provider side of medicine. In my opinion, providers needed to see and understand this concept of value creation, one that went counter to the conventional "treat-and-street" volume-based health system prevalent in the US.

My journey back to the provider side of medicine started in the realm of utilization management–meaning how healthcare providers interact with and respond to insurance payers–but it soon expanded into the world of provider-side care management—the means through which providers guide and assist patients along their healthcare journey. The disjointed nature of how we tend to manage the care of our patients provided a great point for us to lean into efforts at constructing and creating value in the health system.

With my provider colleagues, we built numerous enterprises in the value space using Population Health driven Value-based Care models of care, including a Medicare Accountable Care Organization (ACO), a Medicaid managed care plan through a provider service network, bundled payment structures with the

Centers of Medicare Services, and a vehicle through which to work directly with employers. All of these used a similar framework to manage the care of the people we served. This same framework could be applied to both patients with no insurance or ability to pay and to those with a payer.

It was no surprise that the success of any of these efforts depended on the engagement of physicians and providers. Fortunately, since what motivates most physicians is better patient care and less time spent doing non-physician work, providers generally accept the construct of Value-based Care, once carefully and properly explained. Therefore, though change can be difficult for all folks, along with honest straightforward explanation, education, and support, Population Health Management and Value-based Care made it somewhat easier to guide physicians into the value space. These concepts could not be presented as lofty ideologic concepts or as flavor-of-the-month projects we would later jar up and place on the trophy shelf. The practicality and common sense of value in healthcare needed to be described, and processes and systems meant to support these efforts and the providers engaged in them needed to be built.

I am writing this book not from the perspective of an academic, an economist, or a healthcare policy expert, but as a rural family doc who has seen, worked in, and lived on all sides of the medical curtain. I've seen many examples of what doesn't work and a shining example of healthcare at its best–Value-based Care– which is why I started jotting down notes and writing articles about the topic.

As I was assembling this book from several articles and essays that I'd written over a few years and finishing up the text, the world experienced a global pandemic due to a Coronavirus – SARS-CoV-2, or Covid-19, as we have come to know it. The social and economic changes brought on in response to Covid-19 exposed and emphasized many cracks in our society's foundation, especially in healthcare and social disparities.

The economic impact has been especially telling in most of the healthcare provision sectors, where the reliance on volume and bill-generating encounters by physicians, providers, and facilities was underscored when patients stopped coming in. This caused extreme economic hardship on this segment of the economy, even ruin in some cases, and these entities transmitted their stress and pain onto the patients they served.

On the other hand, healthcare providers who had begun moving toward prospective payment and value-based healthcare have emerged as the exemplars of strength for others to follow. These folks, who now seem prophetic, had simply recognized the unsustainable nature of the conventional healthcare delivery model in the US and instead followed a blend of healthcare found in other parts of the world and some of the concepts of value creation that became buried in the insurance language of the Patient Protection and Affordable Care Act of 2010.

Another glaring fault in our healthcare delivery system was the disparity seen in outcomes of patients who lived with various social risks—poverty, lack of access to healthcare either from a financial or geographic perspective, and so on. Initially, experts thought that simply the presence of medical comorbidities like diabetes, hypertension, heart disease, or COPD were the culprits of these poorer outcomes. Upon closer examination, though, what led these poor-outcome patients to have these conditions in the first place, as well as what allowed other socially challenged and marginalized individuals to be more vulnerable to Covid-19, was the social risks they face daily, risks that we saw in people like Donna.

Numerous stakeholders in the healthcare industry have pointed out how gaps in healthcare services and necessary social and economic support systems have contributed to the disparate experiences of Covid-19 in some communities versus others. They point to data from the Kaiser Family Foundation as exemplary of this, data which shows that in places like Louisiana, African Americans account for 31 percent of the population yet experience over 54 percent of the state's Covid-19 deaths (study done mid-May 2020).[1] This high death rate is not based on a genetic difference but social and geographic differences. Our current, retrospective reimbursement, the fee-for-service model of healthcare, is ill-equipped to address or solve these inequalities and risks.

Though this book was started before the pandemic of 2020, the post-pandemic world makes the concepts presented here even more compelling and essential to both the survival and the optimization of healthcare delivery in the US. Through this book, I hope to define both Population Health and Value-based Care, bring to light value's importance in healthcare, contrast our current volume-based fee-for-service healthcare model to one based on value, and show that value creation is merely the practical application of Population Health Management principles. In doing so, I will introduce the three pillars of Population Health—Risk Stratification, Plan of Care, and Longitudinal Support—demonstrating how they are essentially the three major components of the Value Equation. I will provide multiple examples and applications of Population Health concepts to illustrate how they create value.

> *The post-pandemic world makes the concepts presented here even more compelling and essential to both the survival and the optimization of healthcare delivery in the US.*

All the while, my hope is to demonstrate Population Health and Value-based Care as clarifying perspectives and principles in healthcare, not as disruptors. Physicians and Nurses don't like disruption, and they intentionally avoid things that disrupt their flow. I am optimistic it will become obvious that Population Health Management and the creation of value in healthcare actually support the basic tenets of delivering and facilitating optimal patient care.

However, how money changes hands will be disrupted. Whereas, in our current system, the care that most compassionate and empathic providers desire to give to their patients today is impeded, a healthcare system that creates value, for both the patients and the providers, will remove those barriers, enabling and empowering both providers and patients both to achieve higher standards of care.

Rather than being disruptive, such a change, will facilitate us in our extraordinary task of helping people make their lives healthier.

REFERENCES

1 Steven Ross Johnson, "Covid-19 Highlights Need to Tackle Lingering Social Needs," Modern Healthcare, June 13, 2020. https://www.modernhealthcare.com/safety-quality/covid-19-highlights-need-tackle-lingering-social-needs?

A Coat with Two Pockets

———

THOUGH THIS BOOK FOCUSES on the creation of value in the context of healthcare delivery, it's important to remember why we chose to deliver care, to whom the value is the most precious, and the implications of accepting that responsibility.

The Hasidic Jews had a saying to help them keep perspective of who, and whose, they were. "We need a coat with two pockets," they would say. "In one pocket there is dust, and in the other pocket there is gold." Dust to remind them of their earthly beginnings and gold to remind them of their heavenly end.

Those who care for patients in the medical profession would likewise be well served to "own" such a coat in order to maintain perspective.

> "We need a coat with two pockets. In one pocket there is dust, and in the other pocket there is gold."

Dust symbolizes the mortality of those we serve and of ourselves. It's a reminder of our shared humanity. Our patients are frail, life is a terminal condition, and we, ourselves, are only dust. People move to wellness more quickly and more effectively when they feel cared for. Applied compassion leads to the awareness of "being cared for" rather than merely being "treated," and showing compassion for the unwell is much easier from the empathic position of one's own imperfection and weakness.

As for gold, three meanings and reminders come to mind. The obvious first thought is that the practice of medicine is our livelihood and yields our "gold." Yet for the healthcare provider, gold also represents the honored and respected place we assume or in which those we serve place us.

Those of us who work in the healing art of medicine are members of a royal priesthood. Because of our chosen profession, our earthly companions put us in a place of respect, set apart, and held to higher standards. Because of this respect, we are given authority to see and touch the most private areas of our patients, both figuratively and literally, and we are expected to handle with reverence these most personal and cloistered parts of those we serve.

Finally, the gold in our pocket in this analogy could represent the treasure that is the practice of medicine. This is most closely aligned to the Hasidic perspective of heavenly treasure. The day-to-day practice of our art—listening, healing, educating, and guiding—brings a treasure to those affected by the work:

patients, families, and ourselves. Ask a family member of a patient saved or comforted by a Healer, and they will tell you that such a person—or rather such an experience—was a treasure to them, one they will always carry. When the patient acknowledges that gift to a provider, it is at least as valuable, if not more so, to that person as well.

So, wear your two-pocketed coat with both humility and pride. Be reminded daily of the frailty, faults, and mortality we have in common with those whom we serve, and be open to that fact when interacting with patients. Yet also be reminded of the power we wield and the blessings we can bring into this world, remaining ever mindful of the responsibilities that come with that position–and with that coat.

_____

CHAPTER ONE

Context: Where are We and Why are We Here?

How DOES AN INDUSTRY survive in the twenty-first century when it does not focus on, or even acknowledge value? Generally speaking, the lack of concern about creating value for a customer was overwhelmed and abandoned back in the 1920s, overwhelmed with the advent of advertising to differentiate the multiple brands of a single product, right? That may be true for cars, toasters, and biscuit flour, but up until recently, healthcare has appeared to be immune to the market forces that have demanded that other business segments focus on value.

For most industries, disregarding value while continuing to sustain economic growth is usually short-lived. So why has this scenario persisted for decades in healthcare? There are at least four possible explanations for this phenomenon, either alone or in combination.

The first reason might be the lack of competition in either the product itself or the industry as a whole. In these cases, the product is something that everyone feels they need and there's only one supplier, or the suppliers are limited compared to the demand. Some examples would be the early days of Texas Instrument calculators or cell phones, or all the (short-lived) days of the Pet Rock.

Another great example would be Ford's Model T automobile. Price was the driver in this instance, with quality and customer experience taking the rumble seat. Henry Ford is famously quoted as saying, "A person can buy a Model T in any color they want, as long as it's black." Ford's business model at that time was just to churn out as many Model T cars as quickly as possible, make the sale, and keep on building more cars. Ford's production and distribution models set the standards for mass manufacturing at the time. Eventually, though, people wanted some say in the features and accoutrements of their vehicles. Perhaps corporate healthcare is still in its infancy as an industry.

Competition, or a true lack thereof, in a more mature environment may be another explanation. In many areas, there are few choices for healthcare delivery, especially the acute care services offered by hospitals and facilities. Even between outpatient offices or in communities with multiple acute care health systems, the product being pedaled—namely fee-for-service, transactional, repair shop medicine—is basically the same from one entity to the next. There is talk of brand loyalty with health systems or physician practices, but this "loyalty" is often based on experiences out of the control of the provider ("I won't go to ABC Hospital, because 'they killed' my dad/aunt/sibling/etc."). Additionally, "brand loyalty" is instantly undermined almost every time by an insurance network if the person has health coverage. If a provider or facility isn't in one's coverage network, people generally find another option. More on this when I get to reason number four.

A third reason might be the hubris of the medical profession and healthcare industry. Perhaps we believe that the services we provide are so vital–like public utilities–that people will keep using our services, regardless of our apparent obliviousness to creating value. This notion of indispensability and (this false) sense of invulnerability may have been fueled by the fourth potential explanation…

A disconnect exists in the currency exchange process for services rendered, creating a cushion of ambivalence, or at least opacity, that distracts from the search for value. A customer, by strict definition, is one that purchases a commodity or service.

Over 90 percent of the healthcare in the US is paid for by someone other than the patient. Money, in the form of premiums, is deducted from a person's paycheck (employer), covered by a governmental entity (Medicare or Medicaid), or paid by an individual to a third-party payer (insurer). Generally, this money is held by the payer until a provider or facility submits a bill. The payer writes the check to cover services rendered, and then, after the fact, notifies the patient of the bill and informs them of their portion owed.

Therefore the payer, whether it's an employer, insurance company, or the government, is actually the customer in healthcare. While patients are consumers of healthcare services, they are actually customers of healthcare coverage. Once deductibles and out-of-pocket maximums are reached, a patient rarely hands over a significant portion of the bill's total claim submitted by the provider or facility. Perhaps this distance between the patient's wallet and the provider's hands, as well as the distance between provider, customer, and consumer, blurs the typical financial contract between the provider and receiver of services that would normally demand value for the money spent.

> *A customer, by strict definition, is one that purchases a commodity or service. Patients are actually customers of healthcare coverage.*

From a hospital's perspective in this disconnected world, insurers and physicians can be seen as patient brokers, each exerting influence over the patient as to where the patient will seek services. Not only is the patient's choice of where services will be rendered potentially limited, but the patient is also usually not involved in the building of the approved network and is unaware of the actual cost of the services received. This break in the line of financial accountability may have been the greatest contributor to the ignorance of value in healthcare.

Until recently, providers and facilities would regularly raise prices and insurers would in turn raise premiums, but now this is recognized as unsustainable. Sensing the inability to wring any more premium dollars from employers or patients, insurers have begun trying to find ways of controlling costs or shifting more costs to consumers. Again, though, the money spent by the patients tends to be insurance costs rather than directly handing money to doctors or hospitals. Even with a high deductible plan, the patient cost has more of an insurance feel, and if it's tied to a Healthcare Savings Account, there may be even more of a disconnect between service and payment.

In addition to insurers trying to stretch healthcare dollars in a frenzied inflation of healthcare costs, some atypical, non-insurance company entities have emerged, exerting efforts to bridge the chasm of healthcare funding and payment, and they started to demand value for the healthcare dollars they're spending. Since employee health care expenses have been the fastest rising costs facing employers over the last few decades, and since many organizations self-fund their own health plans–examples of chasm-bridgers who set aside their own money to pay claims–therefore the concept of Population Health emerged beginning in the early 1990s as an attempt not only to lower costs but to increase value overall. It was in these roots of self-funded employer plans, long before the Affordable Care Act of 2010, that the concepts of Population Health Management to create value were developed and refined.

For some background, let's examine at a macro level the concept of self-funded employer health plans. An organization decides (or is required) to offer healthcare coverage to its employees as a benefit. Instead of paying premiums to an insurance company for a "fully funded" plan where the insurance company is on the hook for all expenses, the business decides to self-fund a "bucket of money" through its own contributions plus whatever they deduct from the employees' paychecks, out of which all the medical claims for its employees will be paid. The organization usually hires a Third Party Administrator (TPA) to handle the administrative work of running a health plan, and another company is usually engaged to provide reinsurance, to provide stop-loss protection against large, catastrophic claims.

Given that the organization, the employer, is now on the hook for all healthcare expenses (this is termed "at risk" in the Value-based Care world)–it's directly their money that has to pay the costs–the company will generally desire to achieve two goals in its administration of the plan:

1. They need their employees healthy and at work performing to the best of their abilities. The issues of both absenteeism and presenteeism (gone from work and at work but functioning sub-optimally) need to be addressed.

2. They must have the best value for their healthcare dollars. As with any other investment in their business–raw materials, contracted services, marketing, etc. –they must ensure that their investment in healthcare services is yielding the highest quality, lowest cost, and best experience for their employees.

This second need is actually a longhand version of the Value Equation. We will dive deeper into that concept later in the book, but I'll introduce the construct of value now:

$$Value = \left(\frac{Quality}{Cost}\right) Experience$$

In my work with self-funded employers, I was surprised to learn there were actually two large sub-sets of organizations: those committed to the relationship with and well-being of their employees, and those who merely wanted to check the box of healthcare benefits as cheaply as possible. Why wouldn't both groups of organizations want what was best for their employees?

Some organizations had a firm grasp of the two issues noted above–keep your employees healthy so they are optimally productive and aim for the highest possible value while funding your healthcare bucket. These companies showed a desire to maintain the longevity of their employees' employment and engage them in a meaningful and mutually fulfilling relationship. They recognized that healthier employees were a double victory. The company was more productive, and the extremely expensive interventions associated with poorly managed chronic conditions were minimized or even avoided altogether.

In order to optimize health and well-being as well as to control costs, these entities with which we worked were keen to try non-conventional methods (for the very early twentieth century), such as health risk assessments; smoking cessation and weight loss programs; narrow high-value provider networks; on-site clinics for urgent care; on-site biometric health fairs to check BMI, blood pressure, and cholesterol; shared savings plans with employees when they chose lower-cost care; and "Centers of Excellence" for specific conditions (orthopedic, neurosurgical, cardiovascular), to name a few.

Our partners were willing to spend a dollar or two now in order to save ten, or twenty, or one hundred down the road. When successfully executed, the return on investment was significant over a period of time. One important component was the endurance of the relationship between employer and employee. If the $1 spent by the organization to prevent coronary artery disease in an employee prevented a $100,000 cardiac intervention five, ten, or fifteen years later, both employer and employee win.

The other sub-set of companies always baffled me. They paid for health benefits, but because employee turnover in their organization or industry was high, they weren't interested in optimizing health and well-being. They cared only about cost. Some were "forced" to provide a certain level of benefits to their employees via organized labor contracts, and they merely wanted to meet the minimum. I recall an executive of a hospitality company client saying almost exactly these words: "There's no employee loyalty, so they aren't around with us very long. Why would I want to pay money now to make someone healthier for their next employer next year?"

Perhaps this statement gives some insight into why they had

such high employee turnover, but that's a topic for another book. The bottom line was that they weren't interested in being proactive about investing in the health of their employees, and eventually their healthcare costs rose at a higher rate than our other clients.

The attitude of the second sub-set of employers reveals a potential flaw in employer-sponsored health benefits, whether self-funded or not. If the entity at risk for the cost of the cohort's healthcare is ambivalent about outcomes and/or long-term relationships, its focus will be on the dollars spent today and not on the proactive efforts to optimize health and well-being. With this mindset, over the long haul patient outcomes will be poor and healthcare expenses will be high.

Interestingly, this attitude and perception probably played a role in a weakness of these employers and TPA (TPA = insurance company, as far as the employee is concerned) efforts to tackle the issues of Population Health. People, in my observation, don't trust "insurance companies," and they trust their employers even less.

When the care management companies and TPAs attempted to engage, patients were often suspicious that the only reason the "insurance company" wanted them in a program or to use a certain provider was to save the company money. Since they rarely saw their healthcare coverage paycheck withholdings going down, the cost of the care rendered was not on the mind of the patient. They wanted "the best" and assumed that the "insurance company" was just trying to save money by offering less than the best.

Likewise, when employers tried to collect health risk assessment surveys or family histories of disease, employees would often think the worst: that their boss was going to fire them for having health risks. Others felt the reach of their employer went too far by labeling them as obese or a smoker.

Where our company had the most success in these areas was when the providers themselves were engaged, supported the interventions, and advocated for the programs to the patient. Yet a single "insurer" rarely has enough patient density in a single practice to have much influence on educating providers about programs.

People, in my observation, don't trust "insurance companies", and they trust their employers even less.

The key to creating value in healthcare, as I discovered through this work, is the relationship between the patient and their primary care provider (PCP). Generally, this is a person the patient knows and trusts. Patients feel, and firmly believe, that their PCP has their best health interest at heart. Do people always listen to their PCPs? As a patient and former PCP myself, I can emphatically answer "No!" But the physician's endorsement of a plan, diet, program, or intervention carries immense weight with the patients. Even if they don't agree to the suggestion that day, patients still mull it over, knowing and trusting that their PCP is looking out for them.

This brings up a key point in healthcare: *Provider-led and physician-endorsed activities and initiatives are the most effective at positively influencing health and well-being in most individuals.*

Other nations have learned this lesson of relationship and trust in the provision of healthcare, and they've staffed their primary care forces sufficiently to provide this. For the sake of comparison to the US, let's consider two of the pricier systems in Europe–the UK and Norway.

Primary care has been the foundation of the National Health Service (NHS) of the UK since its inception in 1948. All citizens register with a PCP and use that PCP as their initial contact, or front door, into the healthcare delivery system. These PCPs are paid a monthly rate per patient (so-called capitation) to care for their registered patients, hopefully delivering the care needed to optimize health and well-being at or below that monetary number. They also have the opportunity to earn additional income based on quality outcomes. The PCP practices work with broader teams employed by the NHS to maximize impact of care. Depending on the region, this wider team may include home care nurses; health visitors providing well-child care; and in some cases, midwives, community psychiatric nurses, allied health professionals, and social workers.[1] This multidisciplinary team works to create value by optimizing health outcomes at an appropriate cost.

In Norway likewise, all citizens and residents register with a PCP. Norway's primary principle in healthcare is equal access to services, regardless of social status, location, and income. The state provides national health policy, including legislation and fund allocation, but the four regional health authorities are responsible for providing specialized health care, and the 431 municipalities are responsible for primary health care cost and provision.

In the municipalities' responsibility for primary care, the aim is to improve the general health of the population and to treat diseases and deal with health problems that do not require hospitalization. The General Practice doctors charged with leading primary care work as gatekeepers to specialized care. These providers are paid a mix of capitation fees, fee-for-service payments, and co-payments from the patient, and they work with multidisciplinary teams within primary care which include nurses, midwives, health educators, social workers, and physiotherapists.[2]

Though not perfect in their design or execution, these models allow the UK and Norway to spend less than the US but also to achieve better health outcomes. Based on 2019 health data from the Organisation for Economic Co-operation and Development

(OECD), 9.8 percent of UK Gross Domestic Product (GDP) and 10.2 percent of Norway's GDP is spent on healthcare costs versus 16.9 percent and climbing for the United States. Cost of living-adjusted cost in US dollars per capita at the same time was $3,943 in the UK, $6,187 in Norway, and $10,207 in the US. However, life expectancy is lower in the US, the suicide rate is higher in the US, and US citizens have the highest chronic disease burden by far—double the UK rate and almost the same ratio as Norway. The obesity rate in the US is 40 percent compared to 28.7 percent in the UK and 12 percent in Norway.[3]

It's no surprise that people in these countries enjoy better health and well-being than the US at a fraction of the cost. The countries have removed one layer of payment bureaucracy from the mix, brought a transparent view of the design and goals of healthcare before its representative electorate (who also happens to be the consumer of healthcare), and empowered primary care workers to intervene proactively as a team in the healthcare of their patients.

A Word about HMOs

Some of you older readers or those aware of healthcare's history in the US (if you haven't become distracted by the thought of "socialized medicine") may be thinking "This notion of prospective payments sounds a lot like capitation and the basically failed attempt of HMOs at the end of the twentieth century." You're somewhat right, but there are some important distinctions about Value-based Care in the twenty-first century compared to the floundering of Health Maintenance Organizations (HMOs) in the 1990s.

Health cooperatives and HMO-type organizations have their roots in medical co-ops for workers in nineteenth-century England and had found their way to the US by the early twentieth century. A company doctor was common in many early twentieth-century industries, like mining, though we could argue the potentially dubious motives of company docs in company towns supplied by company stores. For most of the US, though, the concept didn't catch on.

Piecework and the hyper-segmentation and specialization of healthcare had already assumed a prevalent position in the US by that time, though, especially in more urban regions. As early as 1915, the comedic writer Irvin S. Cobb was satirically lambasting the volume-based, bill-generating, over-specialized provision of medical care in New York City. Cobb relates the story of his experience with modern medicine in the Big Apple, first describing how the doctor "took my temperature and my $15," then noting how medicine had changed from the familiar family doc who was always available and attended to all sorts of maladies to a specialized cadre of sub-specialists. He writes:

> This was news to me. It would appear that these up-to-date practitioners just go ahead and divide you up and partition you out among themselves without saying anything to you about it. Your torso belongs to one man and your legs are the exclusive property of his brother practitioner down on the next block, and so on. You may belong to as many as half a dozen specialists, most of whom, very possibly, are total strangers to you, and yet never know a thing about it yourself.[4]

Even in the setting of conventional medicine already being hyper-specialized and focused on generating revenue through encounters and invoices, the seed of health cooperatives and HMOs remained.

The concept of an HMO lived and became rooted most securely in the western US through the shipbuilding and concrete infrastructure entrepreneur Henry Kaiser, as he developed and built the health cooperative that would become Kaiser Permanente in 1945.[5] Kaiser wanted to be the one giving care to his employees and to do so close to their work and in a way that could keep them on the job. Over time, this model included hospitals and clinics, employed physicians and providers who first served

Kaiser's employees, then expanded to include others who wanted to take advantage of this healthcare structure. Yet not many other similar entities survived.

Things changed for HMOs in the 1970s. The Health Maintenance Organization Act, also known as the HMO Act, is a US federal law enacted under President Richard Nixon on December 29, 1973. The act is stated in bill S.14 of Public Law 93–222 and defines qualifications for HMOs. Because of advantageous provisions in this legislation, the number of HMOs dramatically increased from 1970 to 1990, but their popularity waned at the start of the twenty-first century. Many patients and employers were put off by the perception that HMOs' primary focus was on cost containment, which in many cases it was because organizations did not have the technical infrastructure and capability to monitor and analyze quickly and effectively all the necessary data points needed for value creation in healthcare. This perception and failure of the HMOs to create value moved people back to conventional health coverage based on fee-for-service. Kaiser and a few other organizations remained.

Another potential source of failure for late-twentieth-century HMOs could have been the relative lack of resources to build the framework of support and interventions needed to guide patients appropriately in their journeys to health and well-being.

In inflation-adjusted terms, comparing 2018 to the US GDP from 1970, the US has spent almost ten times the amount more in healthcare costs in 2018 than it did in 1970.

From 1960 to 2018, the percent GDP the US spent on health-care climbed steadily, especially after 1970:

Percentage of GDP spent on Healthcare in US

1960	5 percent
1970	6.9 percent
1980	8.9 percent
1990	12.1 percent
2000	13.3 percent
2018	17.7 percent [6,7]

In 2010 inflation-adjusted dollars, the 1970 US GDP was $4.76 trillion, which means healthcare accounted for $0.328 trillion ($328 billion) in spending. The same 2010 inflation-adjusted dollar value for the 2018 US GDP is $17.90 trillion.[8] Thus, healthcare in 2018 accounted for $3.17 trillion in inflation-adjusted terms. Consider that for a minute: in inflation normalized dollars, compared to 1970, healthcare spending increased by 9.7 times (970 percent!) by 2018.

It could be argued that the incentive to add supportive patient services to the provision of healthcare did not exist in the late twentieth century based on the relatively low spend overall. However, now that we are spending twice what the rest of our peer nations are spending—and getting much worse results—and almost ten times what we spent fifty years ago, the volume of money spent for healthcare overall creates a possibility for redirecting

In inflation normalized dollars, compared to 1970, healthcare spending increased by 9.7 times (970 percent!) by 2018.

some of those funds to non-medical, social issues facing our patients, issues that complicate and derail their health. Apparently, the massive total dollars in play in the late 20th century hasn't yet moved us to meaningful change. Keep this in mind, though: If we diverted just 1 percent of the current GDP to social and support programming proven to work, and if with those efforts we lowered US healthcare expenditures by only 2 percent (a very conservative improvement), we'd have an extra $358 billion to spend on other needs like education, improved infrastructure, and affordable housing.

... Back to the Disconnect

The insertion of insurance payers into the healthcare world between the patients and the providers has removed, or at least disconnected, the importance of price and cost from many of the service receivers' minds, i.e. from the patient's mind. The "customer" in US healthcare, the entity with which the physicians must deal, is multiple insurance companies plus the state and federal governments. Meanwhile, there is not one clear voice expressing the goals and design of healthcare delivery, and PCPs are relegated to the scraps and afterthoughts of the healthcare dollar. This disconnect has allowed healthcare to morph into a volume-based industry with relative disregard for value.

This manufactured detachment also influences payers, much like the employers mentioned earlier, to worry strictly about the here and now while ignoring the future, inhibiting true value, and ignoring the long-term health of patients. Given the mobility of patients and the fact that most US citizens not on a government-sponsored health plan change insurance plans frequently, even while staying with the same employer, payers will oftentimes end up making coverage decisions not based on what's best for the patient in the long run, but rather on the economic impact to their more immediate medical loss ratio today.

Hemophilia and its treatment serve as one example. The summer of 2020 saw the US FDA get close to the approval of gene therapy to treat a certain type of Hemophilia. Prior to this option, patients who had needed replacement therapy for active bleeding would need to be in the hospital to receive recombinant clotting factors at a cost of about $10,000 twice a day for five to seven days—$100,000 to $140,000 per treatment. The justification for this price tag may be debatable, but it is one that we as an industry have accepted. Such treatment may be needed numerous times a year for the life of the patient. Many patients benefit from prophylactic dosing on a regular basis (three to four times per week) with a smaller dose, but that doesn't prevent all bleeding episodes. Either way, the patients need to access care often and they spend between $200,000 and $750,000 per year in treatment. Such is the life of some hemophiliacs with multiple trips for care and a very high expense, the bulk of which is usually paid for by insurance.

The introduction of gene therapy in Hemophilia, though, is a game-changer. Now, a single treatment option alleviates the need for any further treatment. This is great news for patients. The conversation around price, though, is a bit disturbing to me. The manufacturer cites the current (and accepted) great expense of current Hemophilia treatment as a justification to propose $3 million as the cost of its gene therapy treatment. Never mind what it might actually cost to produce, the manufacturer wants to base reimbursement on the savings that such therapy would generate over the lifetime of a hemophiliac patient. Let's ignore that for-profit Big Pharma thorn in the side of healthcare for a moment and consider the likelihood of a payer agreeing to cover that type of cost.

For good or ill, most people in the US access health coverage through their employer. The average longevity of a US employee at their employer is somewhere between three and four years depending on the age of the employee. With each employer change, the health insurance payer changes, and it can also change with the same employer. Based on what a patient with Hemophilia would currently spend in a typical year, a patient treated with the gene therapy at $3 million would need to stay with a specific payer from four to fifteen years for the payer (insurance company) to break even on the cost of gene therapy compared to current costs they would save.

While there is no question that the patient with Hemophilia benefits greatly in both health and well-being when the gene therapy is used successfully, the payer is much less likely to reap the cost benefits of the treatment. In fact, because of the mobility of employees between health plans, the payers will probably spend more on the new gene therapy for a given patient than they would on the current therapies during the average timeframe that the patient would be covered under that payer's plan. If the patients are evenly distributed among all the payers and they stay evenly distributed, it will all work out financially (doubtful). Without that level of control (more likely), some payers will lose money in these cases. How will they recoup this shortfall? Increased insurance premiums, of course.

Such is the dysfunctional, misaligned, wrongly incentivized health system we call our own in the US. Prices aren't based on any tangible reality, and we're encouraged to avoid grossly expensive cures leading to improved lives and continue the ridiculously priced treatment with disrupted lives. The priorities are all out of whack meaning systems and processes are not designed with the patients' interests and outcomes as primary consideration.

Another real-life example of this is coverage of Immediate Postpartum Long Acting Reversible Contraception (LARC). When inserted into interested and consenting women a few days after giving birth, LARC has been shown to improve birth spacing and decrease the likelihood of Preterm Birth–a maternity and neonatal event with potentially severe long-term health implications for the baby, health issues for the mom, negative impact on the baby's family, and (by the way) tremendous amounts of money spent in the Neonatal Intensive Care Unit and potentially over the lifetime of the child. Safe, reliable, and effective birth control can help prevent this issue.

The problem is often time-sensitive, though. Some moms get pregnant even before their postpartum follow-up visit. Some are too busy with being moms that they don't come to their postpartum appointment. When moms get pregnant again within twelve months after birth, complications like Preterm Birth skyrocket. Interestingly, almost all payers cover LARC at or after the post-partum visit, but many bundle the expense of LARC into all the services accounting for the hospital delivery fee if done immediately postpartum. This is a disincentive for facilities and providers to perform immediate postpartum LARC, then, because the provider isn't reimbursed for the service and the facility has to eat the $800 to $1,000 charge for the LARC device.

The State of Florida (and other states) realized this and moved to get its Medicaid Managed Care Plans (MMAs) to cover immediate postpartum LARC separate from the delivery, or to "unbundle" it from reimbursement. The concern immediately voiced by the MMAs was the added expense to them with no long-term benefit for the MMAs. Since most moms on Medicaid in Florida were on it strictly for their maternity care, these patients fell off the rolls of membership in the MMAs immediately after delivery. There was no guarantee that when the moms chose to have the LARC device removed and plan a pregnancy down the road, they would be reassigned to the MMA that had already paid for the LARC. Their complaint was they would be paying for a service for which another MMA or even commercial payer (if the mom subsequently changed coverage) would reap the benefit. In my opinion, this is another example of the misalignment of incentives in our dysfunctional system. We've designed healthcare so that in instances like this, doing the best thing for the patient doesn't necessarily make the best business sense for the company, allowing negative effects on quality, cost, and experience, and causing patients to suffer.

The State, though, would benefit in terms of decreased costs, which brings up an interesting point. When healthcare dollars are tied to a specific individual and follow that person, interventions done now to avoid long-term issues later becomes a wise business decision in addition to being the right thing to do. The State of Florida could have changed how they pay for LARC rather than insist MMAs cover it in the immediate postpartum timeframe. Besides the health benefits to patients and their possible unborn children, the State has the most to gain from LARC financially. That's partly why Medicare patients (those over 65, generally) are benefitting most from innovation in the value space at present because once a Medicare patient, you're pretty much a Medicare patient until you die. The patient and the payer (US government via CMS) both benefit from the $1,000 spent on you now that saves $100,000 five to ten years later. I say this not so much as an argument for a government-sponsored health coverage option–though I agree with that concept–as much as a way to point out the disconnect between how dollars are spent and the patients' say in the matter.

As spectators in their own care, patients are oblivious to price; they trust they won't be harmed, but they have no real way to judge quality, and they apparently assume it's OK to be treated the way they are when receiving healthcare in a system designed around the convenience of providers and facilities. In other words, current conventional healthcare offers no avenue to value for the patient.

Quality and experience play no role in a volume model. The goal is simply to keep the folks moving through the system. If they relapse, don't improve, or are actually harmed by our "care," no worries, we can run them through again and bill again for the services rendered. The number of patients you see or procedures you perform is how the money is made, and that volume alone determines how much you make.

This model of healthcare delivery, fee-for-service, and volume-based, has stood since the early twentieth century. Healthcare spending has continued to rise along with the percentage of our GDP spent on healthcare to the point where we are an obvious outlier in the world as regards spending on healthcare. Unfortunately, there is no evidence that this pattern has led the US to a healthier population or to an improvement in our well-being.

In lists of the effectiveness of countries' healthcare systems, the US has continued to drop in the ranks. We are now barely in the top twenty in the world. Meanwhile, our medical spending per capita is more than 20 percent higher than number two Switzerland, and about 50 percent higher than the rest of the world-leading countries.

The financial pressure exerted by rising healthcare costs in the US with no discernable evidence of benefit or return on investment has prompted many people to ask why and to press for answers. Interestingly, the move toward creating value in healthcare delivery has been taken on and promoted in recent years mostly by the payers, the "Middleman" insurance companies. They see the rising costs. The commercial insurance payers understand they can't continue to ask for higher premiums and then ask again. The commercial and governmental entities both realize they are at risk for the healthcare dollars they have at their disposal, and they're trying to do things to create value.

Too bad, as I noted earlier, that no one trusts the "insurance companies."

Over the past few years, some payers have started to figure out this disconnect, and they've been finding ways of inserting themselves into the patient-provider relationship. The United Healthcare-Optum merger has led the way. This company, one of the largest insurers in the country, purchased a vehicle through which to access (and own) PCPs and other providers. Since that merger, Optum has been building the ranks of employed physicians in practices, including the purchase of DaVita, one of the largest multispecialty groups in the country, and the purchase of surgeons and surgery centers.

Aetna and CVS have teamed up to address the issue from the urgent care perspective with CVS walk-in clinics. They hope to leverage those locations into PCP practices, controlling access and medications. The same is true with Walgreens and Humana in the urgent care space, and with Humana's new foray into PCP clinics for senior citizens in their Partners in Primary Care initiative.

In all of these instances, insurance payers are bringing PCP practices into their corporate folds, albeit at arm's length, and transitioning these practices from fee-for-service volume to a value-based model. At the same time, venture capital investors and private investors (often physicians) are following the same model: bring in practices through management or ownership, and transition them into practices that create value.

Hospitals and health systems are taking a stab at this, as well. They have had at least three different surges in practice acquisition over the past thirty years, but none has panned out successfully over the long haul. This includes most health systems presently engaged in trying to transform medicine through PCPs. Unfortunately, over these thirty years, most hospitals and health systems have stayed in the volume and production mindset and model. This stance is not surprising in that most hospitals and health systems are built on and sustained by volume and production: "Heads in beds" as hospital administrators say.

Some health systems have successfully transformed–Kaiser (the one success from the HMO movement of the 1980s and '90s), Geisinger, and Intermountain, to name a few. But the vast majority seem to have difficulty shifting their mindset and committing to a change in approach, specifically a desire to provide value to their patients.

> *"I want to know that the $28 billion we spend on Medicaid in Florida each year is improving the lives of the 4 million citizens we serve. Are we creating value for them?"*
> *—Mary Mayhew*

In the midst of this, along comes the concepts of Population Health. What is Pop Health? How does it fit with Value-based Care? Of course, we want value for our healthcare dollars, but what does that mean? What will we measure?

I think Mary Mayhew, while serving as Secretary of Florida's Agency for Healthcare Administration, put it best when she addressed the Florida Hospital Association's Managed Care

Committee in 2019 regarding Medicaid Managed Care. She simply stated, "I want to know that the $28 billion we spend on Medicaid in Florida each year is improving the lives of the 4 million citizens we serve. Are we creating value for them?"

REFERENCES

1 Martin Roland, Bruce Guthrie, and David Colin Thomé, "Primary Medical Care in the United Kingdom," The Journal of the American Board of Family Medicine, Vol. 25, Suppl. 1 (March 2012), S6–S11.

2 D.S. Kringos DS, W.G.W. Boerma, A. Hutchinson, et al., editors, Building Primary Care in a Changing Europe: Case Studies,Observatory Studies Series, No 40. Copenhagen (Denmark): European Observatory on Health Systems and Policies, 2015.

3 Roosa Tikkanen and Melinda K. Abrams, "U.S. Health Care from a Global Perspective, 2019: Higher Spending, Worse Outcomes?" The Commonwealth Fund, January 30, 2020. https://www.commonwealthfund.org/publications/issue-briefs/2020/jan/us-health-care-global-perspective-2019

4 Irvin S. Cobb, Speaking of Operations (New York: The Curtis Publishing Company, 1915).

5 Kaiser Permanente Website – History. https://about.kaiserpermanente.org/our-story/our-history?

6 Statista.com, Accessed July 17, 2020. https://www.statista.com/statistics/184968/us-health-expenditure-as-percent-of-gdp-since-1960/

7 World Bank, Accessed July 17, 2020. https://data.worldbank.org/indicator/NY.GDP.MKTP.CD?locations=US

8 World Bank, Accessed July 17, 2020. https://data.worldbank.org/indicator/NY.GDP.MKTP.KD?locations=US

Grandpa's Mule

As you read this book, you may be wondering how to introduce and apply value-based principles into your organization. The move from volume to value requires intensive change management on the part of leaders while fully aligning and engaging the frontline staff in this change. My dad tells a story that may assist you in your journey.

My father is an absolute master at telling stories of our ancestry. Though he insists all the yarns he spins are true, the veracity of some have been called into question over the years. Regardless, most of his stories are great and greatly told.

This one surfaced on a recent St. Patrick's Day, and, as I've heard a pastor friend say in the past, "This story will preach." I agree it's an allegory for business management, specifically for working with a team.

Like most Midwestern Anglos, I've got a bit of Irish blood in me (which may also account for some of my father's gift of Blarney). On the March 17th in question, we were discussing our Irish heritage and our primary genealogic link to Ireland–my great-great-grandfather Widdows.

Grandpa Widdows was reportedly a well-known mule trader whose mules were always intelligent, patient, strong, and hardy–as mules typically are. Grandpa Widdows took pride in his reputation and guarded it with tenacity.

One day, though, he met his match. He hitched a fine-looking animal to his wagon full of potatoes and cabbage bound for the market. That day was the first time Grandpa had hitched this mule and driven him. With a click of the tongue and a twitch of the reins, Grandpa, the mule, and the wagon were on their way to market. Things were going well until the mule was to pass through a major crossroads' intersection. There, the mule stopped short and would not budge.

Grandpa tried all the tricks he knew, to no avail. Since it was a busy crossroads, a crowd started to gather, gawking and pointing at the sight of the local "Mule Whisperer" and his defiant mule.

This attention was more than Grandpa could stomach, so he decided to motivate the mule in a rather extreme fashion. He gathered tinder, kindling, and dry wood from the roadside, and he lit a fire under the belly of the mule.

When grandpa saw the mule starting to sweat and stir, he quickly climbed back up onto the wagon's slat-back settee. By this time, the fire had kindled to the point of a blaze, so the mule lurched forward. However, he only went far enough to get away from the lick of the flames. The mule stopped and again dug in his heels. Now, though, the fire was right under Grandpa's wagon.

The wagon soon caught fire, and Grandpa was lucky to scramble down with his life just before the inferno engulfed the wagon, the potatoes, and the cabbage. The wagon and the produce were a complete loss. Frustrated and angry with the mule (and himself), Grandpa unhitched the mule and, with a smack on its hindquarters, sent it away to fend for itself.

The lessons in business management are numerous:

1. (Most obvious) Though it can sometimes take a bit of "heat" to get the reaction needed in a project, don't play with fire unless you're willing to lose the whole project (burn the whole wagon and its contents).

2. Don't let your stubbornness guide your actions. 'Nuff said.

3. Know your team. Don't make your first experience with a new team be one of significant consequence. Those trips will work better when you're both familiar with each other. If timelines are accelerated and push us to

work with an unfamiliar team, be cautious about the lack of familiarity on all parts.

4. Trust your team. Contrary to popular belief, mules are not known for their stubbornness (those would be donkeys). Mules are known for their intelligence, patience, and sure-footedness. There was likely a very good reason the mule was hesitant to take the wagon forward, and that reason, especially in the context of an unfamiliar team, needed thorough investigation. Mules can sometimes sense dangers (snakes, predators, etc.) of which the driver is unaware, and the driver is well-served to take balking seriously. If your team is typically reliable, astute, and rational, explore deeply and address any sense of hesitation on their part.

5. When a change in course may be needed in an organization, Geoffrey Moore, in his book *Zone to Win*, suggests considering the possibilities of the wrong horse, wrong rider, or wrong trail?[1] In this case, we'll say Mule, Wagon, Road.

   - Mule: Perhaps this mule didn't possess the necessary skillset. Train the mule. If there is an intrinsic reason why this particular mule wasn't right for the job, use a different mule.

- Wagon: Did an issue with the wagon prompt the pause—perhaps a structural issue, the load, an uneven shaft, an abrasive harness? Check your organization for structural (and process) issues that may be interfering with your team's work or even causing them to stop in their tracks. Fix what you can or get a new wagon.

- Road: Is there an issue with the road? The team may have sensed ruts, traffic, holes, snakes, or mud and have decided the path was unsafe. Again, trust your team, at least long enough to check out and address their hesitations. If you can't fix the road, consider a detour or a completely different and new path.

6. If you're unsure of your team's abilities and motivations, unhitch your wagon before you get too drastic in your managerial approach (i.e., light a fire). If extreme management measures seem called for, take steps to isolate and insulate your core business from potential negative effects before your project, business, or reputation goes up in smoke.

I wish Dad had told me this story before that time I burned my own wagon trying to get my team moving in the direction I wanted.

REFERENCES

1 Geoffrey A. Moore, Zone to Win (New York: Diversion Books 2015), 56.

—

CHAPTER TWO

Value-Based Care

THE TERM "POPULATION HEALTH" has been used so much in the last decade or so that it's almost become clichéd. What does "Population Health" mean? And how does this concept help us deliver care?

Population Health, or its applied cousin Value-based Care, is likely our best pathway to sustainable delivery of quality and meaningful care to our patients. In combining twenty-first-century technology with the aspects that make patients truly feel cared for and known, measures of clinical quality move all stakeholders in healthcare—patients, providers, places (facilities), and payers—toward an end product that brings benefit to all of them.

In addition to optimizing health and well-being, allowing someone to feel cared for should be the ultimate goal in medicine.

Rendering medical treatment to patients in such a way as to make them feel important, respected, and heard–to feel cared for–is the direction in which we should all aim. To get paid appropriately for achieving that goal makes it sustainable.

To understand the quality and care concepts in the context of cost requires a clear perspective of Population Health and Value-based Care. A common definition of Population Health is "improving the health of a population one individual at a time." Here's another definition of Population Health that resonates with me and many others in the "Pop Health" world:

> **Population Health** is the application of *Value-based Care* principles to a specific *cohort* of the population.

In practical terms, this would mean assessing Donna's community for medical needs and social gaps, as well as looking at her, the individual, for the same issues, and then applying these findings to systems and processes that would mitigate her risks, provide needed support, and effectively guide Donna and the residents of that region on their journeys toward optimal health and well-being.

In both of these definitions, the desire to improve health and well-being on a large scale (in a population or cohort) and the need to address the individual's necessities to achieve that goal are focused on together. At a macro level, Population Health and Value-based Care are driven by standard processes that form a common framework of services, initiatives, mechanisms, and measures for managing care. At a micro level, success is dependent on tailoring a program to meet a patient's specific needs via the available framework. The processes of care can be numerous but standard, whereas the plans of care are infinite and patient-specific.

So, what's a cohort? A cohort in healthcare is any segment or sub-segment of people based on geography, payer source, employer, disease conditions, specific surgical procedures, etc. They have something in common. We can apply the concepts of the framework to patients in groups based on where they live, who pays their medical bills, if they all have diabetes or another chronic condition, or if they're all getting a joint replaced, all of the above, and so on.

In addition to optimizing health and well-being, allowing someone to feel cared for should be the ultimate goal in medicine.

The key phrase in the second definition of Population Health is *Value-based Care*. In general, I prefer the term Value-based Care over Population Health, as it implies sustainable application rather than merely a concept. To understand how this term applies to medicine and healthcare, let's begin with what value means.

The Volume Equation

To explore value, we must first define and consider its contrasting concept, Volume-based Care and the Volume Equation:

$$Volume = Quantity \times Price$$

Volume is a business concept focused solely on production. In this case, an organization is motivated and driven by how many widgets it can produce or "services" it can render multiplied by how much it gets paid for the product/service. A volume mindset, when performed ideally, looks at efficiency: How can you improve the use of commodities to produce more product? However, the Volume Equation also allows for an organization to ignore efficiency to a certain extent if the quantity and the demand for that quantity keep increasing.

Healthcare is a great example of this concept in action, like many organizations which, until recently, have been able to meet or beat budget simply through an increase in quantity demand from aging Baby Boomers. The Boomers' increasing need for healthcare services has brought record numbers of patients through the healthcare doors for encounters, creating bills, and generating revenue. Health systems are able to push more raw material through the line, add production staff as needed, and churn out an increasing number of products.

Yet as "price" (reimbursement per unit) declines, as it has in healthcare in recent years relative to costs, efficiency (meaning an improved rate of patients seen and treatments prescribed) has become increasingly crucial. The volume model views patients, staff, and providers as commodities to be managed and used to keep the volume churning, as means to an end, with the end or goal being higher volume (more patient visits). More on this de-valuing of healthcare's "components" later in the book.

The Value Equation

Value takes a very different perspective from volume in view of performance, one that considers the consumer and the quality of work being done. Whether consciously or intuitively, consumers in most industries make their decisions to consume or re-consume based on value. The Value Equation is a simple representation of a somewhat subjective concept, but its power can be transformational.

$$Value = \left(\frac{Quality}{Cost}\right) Experience$$

Cost (what we pay to produce or consume) is concrete and objective (though price-setting isn't always based on reality). An organization knows its cost (or should know its cost) to deliver a product or service, and consumers know what they pay for that product/service. Ideally, quality, too, would be objective, though sometimes it carries a perspective bias. We can measure experience through surveys or other means, but this component of the equation, one that has a multiplier effect rather than an additive effect, is based on the subjective perception of the consumer.

Whether we purchase a meal, or a car, a vacation, or medical care, we as consumers determine the value of that interchange based on these three components—cost, quality, and experience—and we repeatedly calculate the value of our purchases whether we're cognizant of that calculation, or not. Value doesn't mean cheapness. We're willing to pay more if the quality is great, or we might agree to a product of lesser quality if the cost is low. Meanwhile, an experience that knocks it out of the park versus an interchange that's an annoyance will exponentially change the level of perceived value.

(For the record, let me state now that I really enjoy eating— hence the tendency in my writing to use examples and stories pertaining to food and restaurants. Please don't judge me! Truly, the parallels between food service and healthcare are many.)

We apply, often unconsciously, different parameters to our discernment of value based upon our desired outcome. If I want a quick lunch of a chicken sandwich, a good-tasting sandwich served hot and fast by a friendly person at a reasonable price will create the most value for me. Would I pay a dollar more for friendly service? Probably, but I definitely would pay an additional dollar for the meal to be hot and fast.

If cost is the initial driving force behind my spending decision, two equally priced products will be separated, and one chosen, based on quality and/or experience.

If I specifically want a meal of broiled grouper with mango salsa and risotto, I might tolerate a high price or slow service to get

We apply, often unconsciously, different parameters to our discernment of value based upon our desired outcome.

that specific taste in my mouth. In this case, my sole expectation of a high-quality outcome of the dish drives the equation.

Conversely, if a pleasant dining experience (rather than a specific meal) is what I desire, then I will define value in a different light, beyond just the quality or price of the meal. If the Maître d' of the Grouper Chef's Restaurant treats me like a fool, he seats my party of four at a two-top next to the kitchen door, my waiter is non-existent (except for delivering my tasty fish in a timely fashion), and the person occupying the cubic feet next to our table spends his entire dinner yelling at his cell phone, my dining experience would be adversely affected. I would likely judge the value of the restaurant as low. I probably would have been happier (read: would have experienced higher value) at the

Ethiopian restaurant down the street with a simple lamb dish, pleasant service, and a quiet place to enjoy my companions.

Change of pace: If I am dead set on driving a certain model of car, I'll tolerate a high price and a poor sales experience to get that specific car if necessary. What if another dealership can deliver the same car at a lower price and treat me like a king? I'd choose that one, of course, as the cost and experience would positively influence the Value Equation. When the quality of the outcome is the driving force of the consumer, and there are two or more purveyors of that product or service of similar quality, then cost and experience will drive consumer choice because they create additional value.

You get it. Balancing the interplay of these three components is how an organization defines its value proposition.

In healthcare, these three factors of the value equation can be further defined as follows:

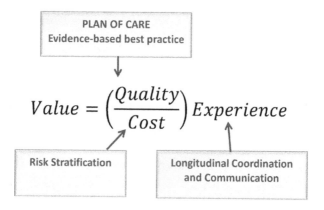

$$Value = \left(\frac{Quality}{Cost}\right) Experience$$

These principles that define Value serve as the Three Pillars of Population Health and Value-based Care in medicine, supported by the appropriate application of relationship and technology.

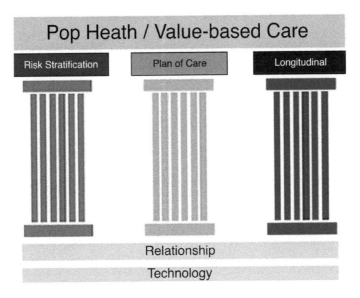

Cost = Risk Stratification

Resources are finite. In medicine, we cannot apply every resource to every patient (we don't have the money, time, or personnel to do that), nor does every patient need or want every available resource at all times. For those reasons, we must stratify patients based on their risks to determine who would most benefit from services in terms of health optimization from the application of our resources. Is this rationing? No. It is good stewardship and appropriate care.

Interestingly, when much of elective healthcare was shut down during the Covid-19 global pandemic, people's use of emergency services for chest pain and other conditions dropped precipitously. People weren't going to the Emergency Department (ED) or their doctors complaining of chest pain or potential signs of coronary artery disease. Heart catheterizations and stent placements also dropped significantly in frequency. The good news is that there was no apparent spike in deaths due to coronary artery disease or other similar conditions. This led some thoughtful physicians, including cardiologists, to declare that perhaps healthcare in general is overused in the US without clear benefit. Certainly, in a system where reimbursement is based on how much volume runs through the door, there is no incentive not to encourage overuse, and the desire to stratify patients according to their risk and potential benefit from a service is not fostered. Give everything to as many people as possible so you can send a bill for the services rendered.

At least four general categories exist for risk stratification, including disease-specific risks, social risks, behavioral/mental health risks, and risk of readmission or adverse event. Ideally, all these areas are screened and prioritized into specific risks for each patient. This allows the caregiver to factor all potential gaps in care, holes, or rough spots in transitions, and obstacles to overcome to be factored into an appropriate and individualized plan of care.

As noted, patients can be stratified based on their specific disease-state (Gold Score for COPD, HEART Score for chest pain, STS Score for cardiothoracic surgery, sepsis risk, etc.), and their Plan of Care can be adjusted to account for their disease risks. This risk assessment and stratification is usually done by clinicians, and since some risks can change or appear quite suddenly (as in the case of sepsis risk), these risks are measured frequently, sometimes multiple times in a day.

We'll spend some time later in the book discussing Social Determinants of Health (SDoH) and Social Risks, but here is a quick overview for this context of risk stratification. The World Health Organization defines SDoH as the conditions in which people are born, grow, live, work, and age. An important and sometimes missed truth is that these conditions can be positive or negative determinants. When one or more determinant has a negative and direct effect on a person's health or on their ability to maintain health, we define that as a Social Risk. Examples include:

- Lack of reliable transportation
- Housing Insecurity/homelessness
- Food insecurity
- Social isolation/lack of caregiver support
- Connectivity (we have many healthcare tools these days that rely on data and mobile services)

- Language translation
- Healthcare literacy
- Access to care
- Affordable meds
- Education/employment security
- Public safety/interpersonal or domestic violence

When we identify individual-level social risk factors, we can devise interventions to address them specifically or collect data to understand where community-level interventions might improve a population's health.

Acting on the results of screening for Behavioral and Mental Health Risks can also greatly affect a patient's Plan of Care, and again, we'll dig into that in more depth later. As an example, for now, undiagnosed or untreated depression in a patient with heart failure (HF) results in at least a two-fold increase in hospital readmission, a doubled five-year mortality rate, and a 30 percent increase in medical costs compared to HF patients without depression. Screening for and intervening in the presence of depression as a comorbidity, in this case, can improve health and well-being (keeping people home, where they're happier, instead of in the hospital), and this will decrease the total cost of care for these people. Win/Win. For example, identifying a patient's risk of suicide and properly intervening, simply put, is a matter of life and death.

Another common risk strati-fication applied by health systems is the risk of readmission after someone has just been discharged from an acute care stay. The world of predictive analytics has afforded us the opportunity to take discrete fields of data—medi-cal, social, geographic, etc.—and *When we identify individual-level social risk factors, we can devise interventions to address them specifically or collect data to understand where community-level interventions might improve a population's health.* combine them in algorithms to determine a patient's risk of an unplanned return to the hospital. The same predictive stratification principles can be applied to a patient before a hospitalization event to determine whether an emerging risk exists for them.

The application of these predictive analytics tools before a hospitalization or event occurs is the "Holy Grail" of risk strati-fication in Population Health and Value-based Care. The con-ventional method of "case management" has been to find the patients that spent the most over the past year and then throw resources at them in an effort to decrease their utilization and cost. As in most cases of business, a reactive approach is less than ideal and yields both a decreased ROI (Return on Investment) and ROH (Return of Health) than a proactive approach.

While there is some merit to working with patients who have experienced a great decline in health and well-being as reflected in their increased medical costs, most research shows that these patients either have conditions that lend themselves poorly to management alteration (chronic kidney failure, late-stage cancer, etc.), or that if left to their own devices, their health and spending will regress to the mean. In other words, stratifying patients on high cost typically leads one to try to influence patients whose course is too advanced to affect cost positively, or patients who were going to spend less the next year anyway. Thus, finding the rising risk patient before they have an event is top of the line stratification.

Finding the rising risk patient before they have an event is top of the line stratification.

Consider the example of two 68-year-old, male diabetic, hypertensive patients, both with documented "well control" of their diabetes per a Hgb A-1c blood test (7.0 for both of them). Mr. A is in a committed relationship, sees his PCP regularly, fills his prescriptions on time, gets his bloodwork done, has access to healthy food and reliable shelter, and is active in his social circles. Mr. B's wife died six months ago, he hasn't been seen by his PCP in nine months, has been late filling his prescriptions three out of the past six months, failed to get the last ordered Hgb A-1c, lives in a food desert, rarely leaves his house, and does not have access to a car.

It doesn't take a genius or a complex predictive analytics platform to discern that without some interventions, Mr. B is more at risk for an adverse event like an Emergency Department visit or a hospitalization. The more we know about patients and then apply that knowledge to our assessment of them, the better understanding we will have of the risks and challenges they face. With that knowledge, we can work with them to overcome those individual and specific issues. Directed action is the key.

There was a time in my career where I was very focused on using risk stratification tools with the highest C-score, a measure of a tool's ability to predict risk accurately. While accuracy is important, it matters very little that a tool's score is 0.85 versus 0.6 if no meaningful action is taken on the insights yielded in risk stratification. Therefore, while acknowledging the need for accuracy, I am now more in the camp of "risk stratify as best you can," because I've learned that the most important component is having resources, programs, and systems available to act on that stratification. Analysis and the creation of actionable insights are useless without action or the means by which to act.

For example, I know of an organization that worked with an incredibly sophisticated and accurate risk stratification engine. Every month it would generate a list of patients at risk from highest to lowest and give this to the care management and Population Health teams for action. Unfortunately, since they did not employ enough members on the care management team—whether Nurse, Social Worker, Community Health Worker, Health Educator— there were only enough employees to engage about half the people on the list. This left the other half, patients who were at risk for adverse events, to fend for themselves.

Likewise, the same organization applied its risk stratification model to hospitalized patients to determine who needed extra help. Some of these patients went to Skilled Nursing Facilities (SNF) for rehabilitative services, but the care management team did not follow the patients there. When the health system with which they had partnered pointed out that these patients were falling through numerous cracks–staying too long in the SNF, services not set up for home after discharge, unknown discharge date, no provider followup after SNF discharge, etc. –the operating partner did finally apply care management resources to the SNFs on appropriate patients. The best predictive analytics tool on the market making the most accurate predictions of who needs attention and services is useless if the resources and programs are not in place to support the patients.

The good news is that risk stratification can also inform the organization as to what resources and programs need to be available and developed. Through the process of Risk Stratification, we can discern where and to whom to apply specific resources in a personalized Plan of Care that will precisely meet their needs and assist us in the proper stewardship of medical resources.

Quality = Plan of Care

In all medical interactions, a provider must determine a Plan of Care for the patient, rooted in evidence-based, best practice medical concepts. To a large degree, adherence to best practice is measurable and objective. Based on a patient's condition or circumstances, the medical community has put in the research work to know what practices have a clinically significant influence on medical outcomes. These best practices range from the simple to the complex, from handwashing to the optimal choice of chemotherapy for a specific patient's cancer.

Following best practices is not cookbook medicine, just as the dinner served in a five-star restaurant is not cookbook food preparation. A combination of basic and complex medical principles exists that needs to be applied and intertwined to the development and prescription of a Plan of Care, and many of these involve specific processes. In addition to the outcome of the service provided, the steps in that process can be measured. The combination of these processes and outcome measures creates a good yardstick for determining quality.

Just as the master chef can't always execute every step in the complex process of meal preparation in a busy restaurant, the provider cannot always execute a complex Plan of Care alone. This requires an Interdisciplinary Team (IDT) to help shape and deliver the plan as envisioned by the provider with the input of the IDT–all disciplines focused on optimizing the patient's health and well-being from their perspective while centering on the individual patient. The provider is accountable for the Plan of Care for the patient, but the IDT is responsible for carrying out the Plan. The chef sets the meal plan, but it's the prep teams, line cooks, and waitstaff that actually execute the delivery of the meal to the customer.

Furthermore, each plan of care, while based on standard practices and processes, must be individually tailored to the specific patient and their needs. These patient-specific needs include medical, social, psychological, emotional, and logistical resources, at the very least. Much like in my patients in Appalachia, these forces can exert such strong negative influences that our medical interventions fall short of success. The best way to know and understand where a patient sits from all of these perspectives is to ask.

Many folks in Population Health have touted genomics as the way to "individualize" care for patients. I think this stance misses the mark. While there is definite value in looking at a patient's specific genome (genetic code) to determine what medications will or won't work for them, this medicalized approach to individualized care falls short. We can't (yet) rely on blood or gene tests to give us the full picture of a patient's needs or circumstances that will affect care. We still need to talk to and be in a relationship with our patients.

The best Plan of Care, though, is useless if it is not communicated and coordinated between all the folks involved in delivering on that plan, including the patient. Often experts will say that what we need in caring for patients are new and better treatments or software platforms, hyper-segmentation and specialization to have experts meeting patients' needs, and/or multiple awe-inspiring

We can't (yet) rely on blood or gene tests to give us the full picture of a patient's needs or circumstances that will affect care. We still need to talk to and be in relationship with our patients.

efforts and initiatives to better care for our patients. Unfortunately, an area that seems too often to be ignored or glossed over is communication and collaboration. Technical advances and transcendent initiatives are great, but if the right hand is unaware of the left hand's actions and intent, we will fall short of our ultimate goal of each patient feeling cared for as they journey to optimize their health and well-being. This brings us to ...

Experience = Longitudinal Support

If no one communicates or coordinates the Plan of Care designed for the patient, the likelihood of proper execution of that plan is slim (an image of blind squirrels and acorns come to mind). In fact, it is because of the non-communicating siloes of medical care we have created that transitions between providers and sites of care can be rough or non-existent and that gaps of care are created by our systems which are plenty wide for patients to fall through, experiencing medical setbacks and harm.

Ideally, there would be one person or entity charged with coordinating the care delivery and communication between the patient, provider, and IDT as it executes the Plan of Care designed for that specific patient. The complexity of the Plan of Care determines how much longitudinal support is needed and who needs to be included on the team. Additionally, the composition of an IDT is dependent upon the specific patient, the expertise and comfort level of the provider, and the availability of resources in the community.

Back when I was in office practice, if I saw a patient with no other health problems or comorbidities who had uncomplicated cellulitis (skin infection), I would write a prescription for an oral antibiotic, instruct in its usage, and arrange for a follow-up call with my nurse to check on progress. For this simple process, the team serving the patient would be me, my office nurse, and the pharmacist, and we would all want to communicate consistent messages to the patient while doing our parts of the plan. Fairly straightforward. I could both devise the plan and lead the team.

Now, consider the overweight, poorly-controlled diabetic patient with cellulitis complicating a chronic wound on their lower extremity. This patient may need IV antibiotics at home or in the hospital, improved glucose control, wound care with dressings or even debridement, hyperbaric oxygen, physical therapy, etc. To carry out this plan, the team, in addition to me, my nurse, and the pharmacist, would likely include a Home Health Agency, an infusion center, therapists, diabetic education, a wound care specialist or surgeon, and so on. This would be a highly complex plan with a bunch of moving parts. Someone dedicated to ensuring coordination of the team is needed.

Musical performance (rather than food) gives an appropriate analogy in this case. Consider a solo violinist. The music is designed for her to play alone–maybe she even wrote the piece–and she has the expertise to accomplish the piece, communicating the musical message to all listening. She leads herself through the piece, or perhaps an accompanist with her.

Add three more players to the violinist–another violin, a viola, and a cello–and you have a string quartet. The composition may be more complex, but a member of the quartet, one of the players (usually the first violinist), is capable of leading the group through the piece, adequately communicating the changes, nuances, and musical emphases of the piece to the other musicians.

This player-led model normally works in classical music until you have seven or more musicians. When the ensemble gets to that size, and all the way up to a full orchestra, a conductor is brought in to keep the group together. Typically, the conductor has not written the piece, nor does she play in the performance. Her sole purpose in being involved is to ensure the desires of the composer and the cues from the principal violinist are communicated to the group, so all are in concert while the music is performed.

In a moderate to complex plan of care and IDT, this is the role of a longitudinal care advisor/navigator/manager–pick your term. The point person for the longitudinal support of the patient didn't write the prescription (though they can inform the principal Provider of issues that need to be addressed with the patient) and they aren't executing the plan–playing the music. Their function is to keep the team on the same page of the plan while the care is delivered to the patient harmoniously and as one ensemble.

Here's why we need a conductor to manage effective communication and coordination of a Plan of Care. Below is an example of a care management "Menu":

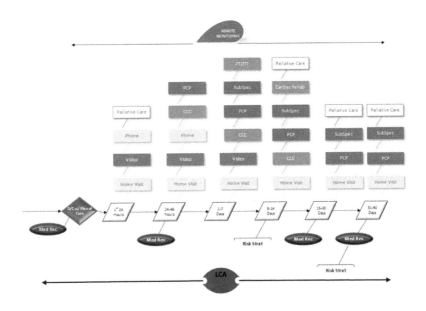

[PCP = Primary Care Provider; CCC = Complex Care Center or "transitions clinic"; PT/OT = Physical and Occupational Therapy; Subspec = Subspecialist, e.g. Cardiologist or Pulmonologist; Med Rec = Medication Reconciliation]

After discharge from the hospital, a patient may need one or all of the services listed. If the patient was an otherwise healthy person admitted with pneumonia, they may only need a PCP visit at seven days, and they're done. If the patient is a hypertensive, diabetic who just underwent coronary bypass surgery complicated by pneumonia, they may need a home visit on day one or two, a video followup in four to five days, a visit with the CV surgeon in a week, cardiac rehab after week two, all while being monitored remotely through Bluetooth devices. That person needs a Longitudinal Care Advisor (LCA) to conduct the IDT orchestra.

Based on the Plan of Care and its complexity, the menu of service options changes. This is where and why technology plays an important role. Even with a dedicated point person, without leveraging technology, adequate, appropriate, and effective communication is a Herculean task which is usually unattainable.

The physical therapist may need to let the pharmacist on the team know that the patient's unsteadiness of gait seems to be related to the dosage or timing of their medication. The community health worker needs to know the plan for physician followup so that transportation and childcare can be arranged. The office nurse may need to refer the patient to a food bank and find out whether the patient followed through. This type of coordination and communication is nearly impossible without an electronic, up to date, editable, asynchronous form of communication that is accessible to the whole team.

On the other hand, if a patient is simply shuffled electronically from one place to the next, even in a seamless fashion, the feeling of being cared for can be lost. In fact, patients can then be left to feel as though they are fending for themselves. "Feeling cared for" is subjective, varying from person to person, but without that sense of relationship and caring, the efficacy of prescriptive medical treatment is greatly hampered.

That's why patient experience is important. Not just because of Governmental Star Ratings, or brand loyalty, or a willingness of patients to part with their money for a good care experience. Rather, positive patient experience has a profound effect on health and well-being. That someone feels cared for should be the ultimate goal in medicine.

> *Positive patient experience has a profound effect on health and well-being. That someone feels cared for should be the ultimate goal in medicine.*

Cures are great, of course, but life is a terminal condition, so we'll always lose the longevity battle. To render medical treatment to a patient in such a way as to make them feel important, respected, and heard—to feel cared for—is a "battle" we can win and the goal for which we should all strive.

At one institution at which I worked, we looked at all the people from the organization who called a patient after discharge from the hospital. The concept of contacting the patient was a good one, but we found that we were overwhelming patients with both the volume of calls and the disparate content of the calls. If a patient with diabetes had been hospitalized with heart failure and COPD, we discovered that they may receive calls from as many as seven to eight individuals, ranging from the facility's discharge nurse to the diabetic and COPD educators, the pharmacist, the heart failure clinic, home health, and many others. Since there was no central, accessible location for a Plan of Care to be read and followed, and no one at the helm of communication, more often than not each caller gave the patient information that differed from that of other callers. This, obviously, led to confusion. Oftentimes, the patient's confusion led to a lapse in care that caused a return to the hospital.

How cared for does a patient feel when they get six phone calls in one day from different folks wanting to discuss their own little portion of the Plan of Care, clueless as to who else is contacting the patient and likely giving contradictory information to each other? How cared for do patients feel if sent out to fend for themselves in the healthcare continuum without being equipped with the necessary self-management tools? Does a patient feel cared for when they're notified a prescription is being phoned in for them, but they don't know why, they don't know what the medication will do, they don't have a ride to the pharmacy, or they don't have the financial resources to pick up the med? How caring are we when we say we'll call them and don't, or we don't even know they don't have a phone?

If we don't know the risks and challenges a patient is facing, we can't develop and deliver on an individualized Plan of Care to meet their health care needs. Without a respectful, meaningful, coordinated, and intentional relationship with the patient providing Longitudinal Support, the "care team" is incapable of rendering effective care.

The essential Pillars of Population Health Management are:

- Risk Stratification
- Plan of Care
- Longitudinal Support

—all built on a foundation of relationship and technology. These are the pillars which will support our patients and shore up the sagging structure of the healthcare industry.

John Wooden's Shoelaces

———

RE-READING JIM COLLINS' BOOK *Great by Choice* reminded me of a story about basketball legend John Wooden and how he set his teams up for success year in and year out.

In a twelve-year stretch at UCLA, John Wooden's teams won ten NCAA National Championships, including seven in a row. His coaching style has been described as simple, consistent, and fundamental, but also challenging and inspiring. The specific Wooden story that caught my attention was what happened (consistently) at the first practice every year, for every member of the UCLA basketball program, players and coaches alike.

Collins has the reader imagine the scene in the UCLA Gym where John Wooden was getting ready to start another basketball season with his team. The top high school prospects in the country join seasoned collegiate All-Americans who've already been crowned National Champions. All are ready to run, jump, shoot, show their talent, and earn their spots on the team. Out comes Coach Wooden and says, "We will begin by learning to tie our shoes."

It's a joke, right? This is some freshman initiation or hazing stunt, right? No. The former champions all start removing their shoes. Everyone in the gym takes off their shoes.

"First, put on your socks, slowly with care, over your toes," says the calm, yet very serious coach. "Smooth out all the wrinkles ... nice and tight ... take your time." The lesson continues through lacing one's shoes and how to tie them.

Collins continues:

> After the lesson, you ask one of the All-American seniors what that was all about, and he says, "Get a blister in a game, and you're gonna suffer. Shoe comes untied in a close game ... well, that just never happens here." One year later, you come to practice, having helped create yet another national championship, noting the surprised looks on the freshmen's faces when the coach announces, "We will begin by learning to tie our shoes."[1]

Tie your shoes right to set up success. It doesn't really matter if you understand the triangle or motion offenses, or the 3-2 zone or man-to-man defenses. If your feet hurt or your shoes come untied, you cannot put that knowledge into any useful or effective practice.

One of Wooden's well-known Twelve Lessons in Leadership is

that "Little Things make Big Things happen," and this shoe-tying story is a great illustration of that. It demonstrates a few important points in achieving success:

1. There are certain basic habits one needs to have to be successful.

2. No one is so talented or successful or important that s/he does not need to maintain these basic habits.

3. Periodic reminders of these basic habits are imperative to the maintenance of success.

4. Failure to exercise the discipline to perform the small tasks correctly can set up large failures.

5. It's the commitment to the successful completion of basic tasks that leads to success, not the dalliance in sophisticated or complex processes.

The translation into the medical world is fairly obvious. Wash your hands. Keep things clean. Follow a pre-procedural checklist. Ambulate the patient. Be kind and respectful. The list of simple, basic tasks required for success in medicine is not particularly long, but failure to execute these shoe-tying steps sets us up to permit complications and failure in our delivery of care, including our efforts to heal with modern, sophisticated treatments. Healthcare veterans may one day say to the newcomers, "Get bacteria from your hands onto or into your patient, and there'll be suffering. Fail to ambulate your patient and you risk ileus or a blood clot. Forget when to use a catheter (or not) or how to care for it—well, that just never happens here."

Wooden's players learned and re-learned shoe-tying every year, and they daily and diligently put that process into practice. Did shoe-tying itself win national titles? No. The UCLA players were still talented and had a deep understanding of the game of basketball. Yet without the disciplined approach to tying their shoes and caring for their feet they would not always have had the opportunity to use their gifts and talents unencumbered by the potential complications of not following through with those foundational practices.

In medicine, we need to have a deep understanding of human wellness and pathophysiology, be skilled at the healing arts, and be able to perform at a top level. However, without daily disciplined attention to the foundational details of practice—hand washing, antisepsis, ambulation, appropriate cannualization, etc.—we allow ourselves to be sidetracked and sidelined by the blisters and loose laces of medicine—wound infections, thromboembolic disease, urinary catheter infections (CAUTI), central line infections (CLABSI), etc.

Likewise, in the value space, we need to exercise the basic principles, the Three Pillars of Risk Stratification, Plan of Care, and Longitudinal Support daily and diligently. Failing to pay attention to any of these areas can cause our socks to wad or our laces to untie. Success in medicine is often less about a new technology, a slick software platform, or a complex diagnosis than it is about securely and effectively executing the basics with diligence and consistency.

"We will begin by learning to tie our shoes."

REFERENCES

1 Jim Collins and Morten T. Hansen, Great by Choice (New York: Harper Business, 2011), 137–38.

_____

CHAPTER THREE

The Real Values in Value

CERTAINLY, THE FINANCIAL IMPACTS of Value-based Care are important: no money, no mission, as they say. However, limiting our view of value simply to metrics of quality and cost of care delivered, multiplied by results of measured patient experience, ignores the revolutionary capabilities of assuming a value approach over one of volume. We need to ask if we're realizing all the value of Value-based Care and not neglect the transformative power of moving from volume to value.

To create true value, an organization must first value the components of the process—in this case, the patients, staff, and providers. For without striving to improve the perceived value of patients, staff, and providers, in our eyes and theirs, the other objective measures of value will likely fall short.

To flesh this out, let's re-examine the Volume and Value Equations and how their components speak to what's valued and what's taken for granted.

Consider the Volume Equation:

$$Volume = Quantity \times Price$$

It is based strictly on how many widgets you can produce or "services" you can render multiplied by how much you get paid to churn them out. A volume mindset, when performed well, looks at efficiency–how can you improve the use of commodities to produce more product? However, the Volume Equation also allows for an organization to ignore efficiency to a certain extent, as long as the numbers are heading in the right direction (i.e., through your door).

Many healthcare organizations, since the turn of the twentieth century, have been able to continue to meet or exceed their budgets simply through an increase in demand. Baby Boomers' increasing need for healthcare services has brought record numbers of patients through the healthcare doors, creating bills, and generating income. Run more

> To create true value, an organization must first value the components of the process.

raw material through the line, add production staff as needed, and churn out an increasing number of products.

Yet as "price" (reimbursement per unit) declines, efficiency becomes increasingly important. In this model, the factors affecting your quantity–patients, staff, and providers–and how you're able to move things through the production line are viewed as means to an end, with the end being higher volume resulting in increased revenue. Patients, staff, and providers are commodities to be managed and used to keep the volume churning.

All of this falls apart, though, in a pandemic setting (as with Covid-19) when patients stop coming through the doors either to make way for the acutely ill (who, in our current volume model, do not bring in as much revenue as elective surgical procedures) or for fear of getting sick. During the global pandemic, just a few weeks without "non-critical" procedures or office visits not only meant we had close to zero patient encounters but also highlighted the cracks in our healthcare system based on volume. If the churn and burn stops churning, the revenue stops short and hospitals and physicians are furloughing employees and are asking for government financial support and intervention.

Contrast this to the Value Equation.

$$Value = \left(\frac{Quality}{Cost}\right) Experience$$

Here, price and quantity are not the multipliers; experience is. How the customer feels about the process is a key component. If expectations are not met, it's hard to create value. It is the meeting or exceeding of these expectations that move customers to part with their money.

In the Value Equation, cost, not price, is key. Since experience drives what the consumer is willing to spend, the entity must focus on what it costs to manufacture or deliver the product or service to the customer. The cost needs to be appropriately proportioned to the customer's experience and the delivered quality of the product.

In value, quality plays a dominant role. Most healthcare consumers assume quality. They expect their providers to get them from point A to point B in the healthcare journey without complications, adverse events, side effects, or mistakes. People expect "Zero Harm," so that's the quality baseline at which we should start, not the goal for which to strive.

Creating value depends on creating a culture that is rooted in quality and supports an excellent experience. It is the people within the organization that deliver on the promises of quality and experience. Through the recognition of the critical role played by folks involved in creating value, these stakeholders are not treated as commodities; rather, they are respected as individuals of the greater whole.

In healthcare vernacular, a volume-based mindset focuses on a churn-and-burn, treat-and-street mentality. If your first efforts at diagnosis or treatment fail, no worries, the patient will be back and you can send another bill, make another collection, and add to revenue. Throughput of patients and capturing all billable services and diagnoses are the priorities. Patients are widgets and the staff and providers are merely cogs and commodities in the machinery of healthcare delivery. Churn out the widgets and simply move around the cogs and commodities as needed to improve production. Though I wish we had have moved past this mentality in healthcare, I still

Most healthcare consumers assume quality...People expect "Zero Harm," so that's the quality baseline at which we should start, not the goal for which to strive.

hear administrators discussing patients as "heads in beds" and nurses and physicians as "a dime a dozen."

The volume model pays no attention to value. Neither the value of the care rendered, the value of the patients, nor the value of the caregivers (staff and providers) plays any role in building an organization around volume. Unfortunately, the volume model is where healthcare has been in the past many decades, and that's a large hurdle we must clear if we are to improve healthcare processes and outcomes and move to create value.

Entities that pay most of the healthcare costs–employers, insurance companies, the government–have had enough of the volume model. Should we be surprised they want value for their US healthcare dollar—a dollar that currently goes the least distance in providing good outcomes compared to all of our international peers, yet is doled out by the payers in higher volume than anywhere else in the world? The market demands value. It demands excellent outcomes at the lowest possible price with a positive experience. Other markets demand these principles, and so should healthcare.

A focus on achieving high-quality healthcare at an appropriate cost while ensuring that the patient's experience is exceptional should also result in the patient feeling valued. A key principle in Value-based Care is this: pro- *Processes are based on cohorts but Plans of Care are based on individuals.* cesses are based on cohorts but Plans of Care are based on individuals. We need to build standard processes for delivering care, but the plans and paths for patients are not necessarily uniform. An un-valued patient (person) will simply be pushed through a standard process, whether it meets their need effectively or not.

The transactional world of volume doesn't care about individuals. Value, though, is relational, not transactional. A relationship must be nurtured with patients to understand their unique challenges, their desires, their goals, and their definitions of health and well-being. Engaging in such dialogue and relationship-building leads a person to feel valued as an individual, not as simply a widget in the production line. As Atul Gwande said in his insightful book Better, "In (the) work against sickness, we begin not with genetic or cellular interactions, but with human ones."[1] Therefore, human interaction is necessary to lead us to the wisdom of how to help one person navigate their personal challenges and, in the process, feel cared for.

Donna and her family needed the relationship provided by the mission workers. The home health nurses knew everything important about Donna and included that knowledge in their interactions. They anticipated Donna's needs and proactively addressed them. Their mere presence in the home gave Donna the secure realization that they cared. If, while in Appalachia, my clinic had built out the world's finest diabetes and heart failure clinics but only saw patients who could come to us in our building, Donna probably would not have benefitted. In fact, she likely would have felt unvalued and left out. Not only would she miss the benefit of the care rendered in the clinic, she likely would have had some despondence or depressive symptoms as a result of our disregard.

Some recent works in healthcare management suggest

segmentation or even hyper-segmentation as a cure for our ailing health system. They list the benefits that patients glean when they are working with specialists, subspecialists, or hyper-subspecialists in the particular issues or conditions affecting the patient. Technically, this is not a new concept, as sub-specialization has been a driver in medical training and healthcare delivery since the early twentieth century. Benefits, of course, exist, in that patients can be managed by an expert in the particular concerns. The problem is not that we don't have enough hyper-focused experts in healthcare. The issue is communication and coordination of the efforts. Without communication and coordination between these segments, we experience the siloed, broken, gap-filled world within which we currently function.

Integration via communication and coordination, not segmentation delivered in isolation, is what patients need. Then not only will all the right treatments be prescribed, but they will also be adequately communicated to the team and the patient, regardless of their level of specialty, detail, or complexity. When the patient sees that all the medical players are on the same page in the care they are delivering, the levels of confidence and comfort rise. This facilitates a sense of being both worthy and cared for.

So when a person feels valued in the delivery of health care, they likely will feel cared for and worthy. These feelings cultivate fertile ground for a patient to experience empowerment and to be engaged, facilitating a journey of self-management of health and well-being. Optimizing health and well-being is much more possible with patients engaged in self-management of their chronic conditions. Helping people see their own worth and reminding them of that worth frequently will get them engaged in addressing all issues they face, especially those of their own health.

Integration via communication and coordination, not segmentation delivered in isolation, is what patients need.

The pursuit of value yields a very different message to our patients than does a focus on volume. In volume, patients are numbers, whereas in value, they're people. Volume is an episodic transaction, but value is a longitudinal relationship. Volume healthcare holds problem-oriented rescue as its theme, while in value, individually focused longitudinal support rules the day.

People (patients) know when they're a number versus when they're a person, and they respond to each designation predictably.

Providers and staff are no different. When volume is the focus of our care delivery, much like the patients, the providers and staff also become commodities and components in the gears of the healthcare machine. If staff members and providers are treated as property and a means to an end, why would we expect them to treat patients any differently? Why would we expect engagement and creativity from something that's simply an apparatus to be manipulated?

In order to achieve value in the metrics of care and to demonstrate the worth of our patients, we must also daily and intentionally demonstrate the value inherent in our staff and providers. Of course, we need standard work and routine processes for an organization to function efficiently, but again, standard does not mean uniform.

Dr. Neev Neuwirth writes in his book *Reframing Healthcare* that valuing employees leads to "engagement, enthusiasm and energy."[2] In turn, valued employees and providers create an environment that facilitates the creation of valued patients. Both of these are essential components in our measurement of the delivery of value. If we strive only to meet outcome metrics and reduce the total cost of care, we're likely going to fail at creating value, and in the process, we will alienate patients, staff, and providers.

If staff members and providers are treated like property and a means to an end, why would we expect them to treat patients any differently?

To create value successfully, we, as leaders, must recognize the inherent worth and importance of both the patients we serve and our colleagues who serve them. We need to view quality and "Zero Harm" as the baseline, not the target. As we let these cultural changes take root, we then need to focus our efforts on improving the experience of all stakeholders involved in healthcare–patients, staff, and providers. It is through the positive experience of all these stakeholders, through them all feeling heard and cared for, that we can then have a multiplying effect on our aim to create value.

REFERENCES

1 Atul Gawande, Better (New York: Picador, 2007), 82.

2 Zeev Neuwirth, Reframing Healthcare (Charleston, SC: Advantage, 2019), 89.

Gift Card Example

———

I KNOW OF A MEDICARE ACCOUNTABLE Care Organization (ACO) that gave patients gift cards as a token expression of value. It was part of their program designed to encourage patient engagement and graduation from its care management programs, and it targeted patients with chronic conditions in need of guidance toward self-management.

This ACO's leaders knew the potential value of its care management program for patients with chronic conditions who graduated the program by gaining the ability to self-manage, both in terms of improved health and quality outcomes for its members and in improved financial metrics due to a positive change in patient healthcare utilization patterns. They discerned that if they could engage more patients whose risk stratification deemed them to need this program and then shepherd those folks through to completion, gaining the ability to self-manage, then these patients would be and feel healthier and the ACO's bottom line of total cost of care would improve. When the Center for Medicare Services (CMS) introduced a new ACO benefit enhancement to encourage the use of chronic care management, the ACO quickly applied the enhancement to its complex and chronic care management program.

The plan was to incentivize patients to engage in and complete the program by giving them a $50 gift card to a grocery store chain upon completion—something very simple and fairly easy to administer. Though the addition of the $50 incentive didn't appear to increase engagement over seven months, it did encourage an increase in graduation by about 15 percent. Translated to patient lives, this was an increase of 37 graduates in seven months. The ACO had previously calculated that every patient that completed the care management program saved the group $4,000 each. So, not only did the lives of 37 patients improve, their graduations likely led the ACO to a $150,000 decrease in overall total cost of care—a return on investment of almost ten to one!

Providing the incentive of a monetary gift card did more than create value through improved quality and decreased cost. Applying a dollar value to completion of the care management program exhibited the importance of the program to the patients (and providers) in a tangible way. It helped frame the significance of the program such that it encouraged the patients to invest their time and energy in its completion, leading to improvement in their health and well-being. People will usually only invest in something that holds value for them. The incentive helped patients realize the worth of their health and act on that realization.

Pepper Shaker Parable

——

THE CONSIDERATION OF AN individualized approach to a Plan of Care, taking the unique and special needs of that particular patient and family into account, dovetails well into a discussion of experience.

Over the past decade or so, patient "satisfaction" has gradually changed to the notion of "Patient Experience," and it is measured mostly through survey. The most common tool is the Hospital Consumer Assessment of Healthcare Providers and Systems, or HCAHPS Survey. These surveys are sent to patients after services are rendered. They are meant to judge the quality of experience, and payors like Medicare and Medicaid base quality payments (or penalties) on these scores. Measuring experience is a key component to discerning whether and how much value is being created. Understanding and delivering on patient experience, though, seems to be a very steep hill to climb for most facilities and practices.

Recently, as I was also considering HCAHPS scores and patient experience, I read an article from Cleveland Clinic about how empathy on the part of a physician can be an effective catalyst for improving patient satisfaction.[1] Empathy, of course, is the ability to understand and share the feelings of another. The article suggested asking a question or making a statement that would signal to patients that the physician saw them as fellow human beings. (It can be hard for patients to feel empathy from a cyborg.)

I considered the thought of empathy a bit further and wondered what level of satisfaction physicians may feel with their experience if they were in analogous circumstances to our patients and regarded the way we often handle our patients. Could physicians empathize with their patients more if they could better understand the concerns and frustrations of those patients in situations of vulnerability and service? Much has been written about the doctor as a patient, but we might avoid hospitalizing all physicians for the epiphany of empathy if we consider the perspective of someone receiving any type of service and care.

As a foodie, for me, of course, the analogy is an evening at a nice restaurant.

Now, I'm fully aware of the articles describing the most satisfied patients as the ones with the highest morbidity and mortality due to getting everything they ask for, and I quickly bring that up in discussions about "satisfaction."[2] I'm not talking about physicians playing Deli-Doc and just giving patients what they order to satisfy their every whim and desire. Instead, I'm talking about guiding the customer to a satisfying experience, with all the communication, coordination, and consideration that entails.

Could physicians empathize with their patients more if they could better understand the concerns and frustrations of those patients in situations of vulnerability and service?

None of us necessarily wants to be judged on how we make someone feel, but the reality is that patient experience scores are likely going to remain an important healthcare delivery metric and even an important metric of patient health. Also, if we want to include Experience in the Value Equation—which is a must—we need to be able to measure the patient experience in some way.

Isn't part of our job as healers to guide patients to the point of feeling cared for?

Most of the people who go to a nice restaurant stay for a full meal, and they rate the restaurant and its servers on the entirety of the experience. There are some folks who just pop in for a quick drink or dessert, and some who stay for hours, requiring multiple bottles to be uncorked and even a tableside flambé, but most stay for around three to four courses. Similarly, some people briefly touch on just the periphery of healthcare while others are immersed in it for weeks. Most stay about three to four days.

If you or someone you know or love has ever received care in the hospital, you know that continuity and communication are rarely a strong suit in healthcare. Would we tolerate that in a restaurant?

Let me tell you a parable.

A customer presents to the host stand at a local restaurant around 5 pm. After being triaged for his needs and discovered to be someone in need of dinner, he is seated at a table. A waiter arrives, presents the evening's specials, and asks for the customer's drink order. The customer states he feels like fish tonight, so the waiter recommends a nice glass of Chardonnay. The waiter disappears.

A different waiter emerges at the table with a glass of water and some bread. She likewise proceeds to tell the customer of the evening's specials. The customer states he's already been told the specials, and he's ordered a glass of wine. The waiter explains she has reviewed his history and he should drink water instead. She also notes that he has ordered chicken in the past, so is he ordering chicken again tonight?

He explains he feels like fish, and in fact, it looks as if the grouper on the menu would suit his needs. The waiter takes his order and states she'll return with his salad.

Minutes later, a third waiter arrives at the table with a salad. He offers ground pepper, but the customer declines, explaining he doesn't care for pepper. This waiter also notes the customer's history of ordering chicken in the past. The customer again states that he feels like fish tonight and has ordered grouper. "OK," says the third waiter, "but since you've had chicken in the past, I will have our Poultrologist pay you a visit."

Midway through the salad, a fourth waiter comes to the table. She, too, is carrying the pepper grinder. She states, "I noticed you have no record of pepper utilization during this stay. May I put some ground pepper on your salad?" The customer explains it's already been offered, and he has already declined. The waiter goes on to say, "I see you've ordered the grouper from the menu. I'm not convinced that dish will meet your needs tonight, so I'm going to ask our Pescatarianist to swing by for a consult."

After the salad, but before the main course was served (because it actually had not yet been decided on by the staff), the Poultrologist comes by the table. Following a discussion with the customer about chicken and other fowl, the Poultrologist declares, "This dinner really has nothing to do with your previous taste for chicken. I'll leave a note for your Primary Waiter to that effect, but please, if you start to feel like chicken tonight or in the future, call me here at the restaurant or come by."

Almost immediately, the Pescatarianist arrives. "I understand your Primary Waiter thinks you want the grouper from the menu," she says. "While I agree that grouper is the right choice for you, I'm concerned the grouper on the menu may not be adequate. To satiate your hunger faster, I recommend we add the mango salsa to the plate. I'll leave a note for your Primary Waiter."

Finally, a previously unknown waiter arrives at the table with the grouper, including the mango salsa. "Would you like ground pepper on that, sir?" the waiter asks. "No," is the customer's reply.

The grouper was magnificent, and though he scraped some of the mango salsa to the side, the customer found that satisfying as well. No one checked in on the customer during the main course—to his relief. The plates were cleared.

Time for dessert. The second waiter returns to the customer's table. She offers the dessert choices but suggests he order the fruit plate. He orders cheesecake and a cup of regular coffee. A sixth waiter returns to the table with a cookie and a coffee cup. "We discussed your case, and we determined the best choice would be this almond cookie. Also, we determined decaf was a more appropriate choice for you, so that's what I brought. Oh, and as an aside, we really think you should eat more pepper."

"Is this negotiable?" said the customer.

"Of course!" said the waiter. "Everything's negotiable. We

didn't realize you'd want to be included in the decisions. I can call a team conference later and we can all discuss your dessert choices with you."

"Never mind," says the customer," I'll have the cookie and decaf."

The customer finishes dessert (truly a good cookie, mind you), pays his bill, and is finally on his way home by 11 pm. He gets a survey later that week, asking to rate his experience.

Consider this encounter in light of some of the HCAHPS questions that patients are asked (paraphrased for food service):

- During this restaurant stay, how often did waiters treat you with courtesy and respect?
- During this restaurant stay, how often did waiters listen carefully to you?
- During this restaurant stay, how often did waiters explain things in a way you could understand?
- Before giving you any new food or beverage, how often did restaurant staff tell you what the food was for or how best to eat it?
- Before giving you any new food or beverage, how often did restaurant staff describe possible side effects in a way you could understand?

- During this restaurant stay, staff took my preferences and those of my family or caregiver into account in deciding what my dinner needs would be.

Of course, patients should not be ordering and dictating all of their own treatment. However, they are keenly aware of our inability to communicate with each other, our inconsistency in communication with them, and yes, even our ignorance regarding their thoughts and wishes. They clearly see how we waste their time and how we are oblivious to their feelings. The fact that we change providers on them without giving our names, much less developing a relationship, is not lost on them, either. Simply calling them sir or ma'am doesn't negate our condescension.

And we wonder why our HCAHPS/patient experience scores are low. We need a super-sized order of empathy to enhance Experience.

Do you want ground pepper with that?

REFERENCES

1 Debra Shute, "The ROI of Patient Experience," HealthLeader, August 1, 2017. https://www.healthleadersmedia.com/finance/roi-patient-experience

2 Joshua J. Fenton; Anthony F. Jerant, MD; Klea D. Bertakis, MD, MPH; Peter Franks, MD, "The Cost of Satisfaction; A National Study of Patient Satisfaction, Health Care Utilization, Expenditures, and Mortality," Archives of Internal Medicine, 2012; 172 (5): 405–411.

Kenneth G. Adler, "Does high patient satisfaction mean high quality of care?" Family Practice Management vol. 23 no. 3 (2016): 4.

———

CHAPTER FOUR

Social Determinants of Health (SDoH) as a Vital Sign

THE MENTION OF SOCIAL Determinants of Health (SDoH) has become so ubiquitous in medical management conversations these days that no dialogue or conference seems complete without its discussion. Vendors and developers have seized on this concept to promote their products as the next great thing because of how their product addresses SDoH. Indeed, SDoH has possibly eclipsed "Population Health" as the trendy buzzword in all things healthcare.

I say this not to jest about or minimize SDoH and their impact on health. On the contrary, the apparent widespread acceptance of social factors having determinative influence on our patients' health and well-being is game-changing in how we deliver health-care services and support our patients. We need to embrace this!

As mentioned earlier and as you've all likely heard, the World Health Organization defines SDoH as conditions in which people are born, grow, live, work, and age. These conditions *can be positive or negative.* I am the beneficiary of numerous positive social determinants, including growing up in a stable, relatively affluent home, an education that facilitated literacy, I have reliable transportation, food and housing security … the list goes on. Many others, like Donna and her family, are not so fortunate.

Given the possibility of positive or negative impact from SDoH, the concept of discerning the social determinants which are influencing a patient's life, health, and well-being is akin to measuring and assessing the physical vital signs we measure in patients—pulse, blood pressure (BP), respiratory rate, and oxygen saturation (O2 sat).

These physical vital sign measurements can be reassuring and positive, signaling to the provider that all is well. Conversely, they can reflect areas of concern, even emergently, when they are outside of the "normal" range. An abnormal BP or O2 sat immediately gets our attention, calling us to assess what's causing the aberrance, evaluate how these abnormal vital signs are impacting our patient and her overall prognosis and condition, and to act quickly to mitigate or remove the issues causing these abnormal findings.

Social Determinants of Health should be a vital sign we assess on all patients.

We assign terms like hypotension, hypoxia, tachycardia, and such to abnormal physical vital signs findings in blood pressure, oxygen saturation, and heart rate, and these terms lead us down well-worn, standard therapeutic pathways to address them. The same needs to hold true for SDoH.

Hugh Alderwick and Laura Gottlieb wrote a great paper about our SDoH lexicon and how we could better apply terms to meet our therapeutic needs in addressing SDoH.1. Much as we discuss physical vital signs, we must attend to SDoH when they present risks to the patient—risks like social, behavioral, and mental health, all of which pose distinct patient problems with separate and unique paths to resolution. When discussing SDoH, as Alderwick and Gottlieb note, we would be better served to use the terms Social Risk Factors and Behavioral Risk Factors. And as they note, Behavioral and Mental Health can be a confounder of behavioral risk. Given the profound comorbid and social pressures applied in these conditions, I've added Behavioral Health Risk Factors to their suggestions, a nod to the old term psycho-social determinants of health.

Below is a list and description of each of these areas of risk:

Social Risk Factors—Specific adverse social conditions/circumstances that are associated with poor health or health outcomes. Any individual-level SDoH that increases one's likelihood of poor health can be referred to as a social risk factor.

EXAMPLES:

- Lack of reliable transportation
- Housing insecurity/homelessness
- Food insecurity
- Social isolation/lack of caregiver support
- Connectivity (we have so many healthcare tools these days that rely on data and mobile services)
- Language translation
- Healthcare literacy
- Access to care
- Affordable meds
- Education/employment security
- Public safety/interpersonal or domestic violence
- Racial discrimination

By identifying individual-level social risk factors, providers and health systems can devise interventions to address them specifically and/or collect data to understand where community-level interventions might improve a population's health.

Betty (Donna's daughter and caregiver) is a great example of negative Social Risks. In addition to genetic risk factors for chronic conditions like hypertension and diabetes, her nutrition was adversely affected by the food desert in which they lived. Their lack of reliable transportation, due to income insecurity, made it difficult for her to seek medical care. Though she loved her mother and was proud to care for her, Betty also suffered the disadvantage of social isolation. Finally, Betty was a smoker, which leads us to …

Behavioral Risk Factors—Individual behaviors (choices) that negatively affect health, such as tobacco use, alcohol use, lack of seatbelt use, dietary choices, etc. Habits that cross the line into Behavioral or Mental Health diagnoses would be included in BH Risk Factors (below).

There is some cross-over here since a person raised or living in a tobacco environment is more likely to smoke, and other social risks may make one more prone to other risky behaviors. But overall, these risks would constitute choices rather than circumstances.

Behavioral Health Risk Factors—Behavioral and Mental Health conditions negatively affecting and being affected by a person's overall health.

Includes Depression, Anxiety, PTSD, Eating & Personality Disorders, Substance Use Disorder, and Serious Mental Illness [e.g., Severe mood (Unipolar & Bipolar) disorders, OCD and the psychotic disorders].

These can be solitary or comorbid with other chronic conditions, either in a primary or secondary role (e.g., schizophrenia + diabetes or heart failure + depression, respectively).

Again, cross-over exists. Is the patient socially isolated due to Major Depression or lack of reliable transportation? Are they malnourished because they don't have access to food or because of Substance Use Disorder? Is the Substance Use Disorder based in a trauma related to one or more social risks? Determining the **root cause** of the presenting sign will direct appropriate care–again, much like the assessment and treatment of abnormal vital signs. Is the high heart rate the primary problem, or is it the result of inadequate oxygen supply or fluid volume in the body? Taking the time to tease out the root cause will appropriately guide the most appropriate individual Plan of Care for the patient.

Consider Donna's grandson Michael's circumstances. He was debilitated by depression. Though a biochemical reason certainly existed for this condition, how much impact did his social situations play? There were few if any employment options for him, and his financial situation, living up a holler, made building a social network very difficult. Would addressing his environment have improved his depression?

(And a bonus ...) Social Needs—Emphasis on the patient's role in identifying and prioritizing social interventions to their risks. This concept is at the heart of efforts that involve shared decision-making. Understanding the patient's values and his application of value to his condition or circumstances, along with the physician's clinical expertise, enables physicians/providers to make well-informed decisions about the appropriate plan of care in concert with the patient.

In other words, what we may identify as a potential Social Risk in a particular patient, they may either not see as such or may be a different priority for them. Directing efforts to the issues high on the patient's priority list will be more effective and less paternalistic. If a particular issue is negatively affecting the patient more than they realize, then it is appropriate for the caregiver to invest time and energy in relationship-building and education, so that the patient gains insight into the issue and develops the desire to address it.

These distinctions, as noted, are indispensable guides for health systems as they tackle the risks their patients are facing. Which areas of risk mitigation should a health system address in order to take the lead in solving problems versus acting as an expert resource to the larger community? A hospital or health system could take it upon themselves to bring fresh food to a food desert, either on its own or in conjunction with an existing food bank. It could also serve as an expert resource to city planners or legislators in discerning how best to meet the needs of a community through store placement or allowance of farmers markets and such. Some issues can and need to be addressed at the individual level, while others may require community-wide or even policy/legislation solutions. These distinctions will likely be different from one community to the next.

The strategies for addressing Social Risks (housing, transportation, food, income, etc.) are different from addressing Behavioral Risks (smoking, alcohol use, seatbelt and helmet use, etc.). From a health system and cost perspective, Social Risks are better addressed on the patient or cohort level, whereas Behavioral Risks can be addressed in the broader population, Public Service Announcement style, as well as on an individual basis or in terms of public policy and local spending.

Feeding or transporting a specific patient or cohort of patients can be a much better use of a Health System's resources than trying, single-handedly, to improve food security in the entire region or trying to fix the public transit system for a community.

Steps specifically to address homelessness or housing insecurity in patients with chronic conditions or recent hospitalizations may be an appropriate area for a Health System to lead in the solution, but tackling the dearth of affordable housing in an entire area may be best tackled by a health system working with or being a resource to a governmental or social entity's lead.

For Donna, the mission chose to apply its home health resource and physician to mitigating some of her social risks. The pharmacy deliveries, house calls, and home care sidestepped her transportation issue and financial woes (to a certain degree). From a nutrition standpoint, we could have taken healthier food to her, or the mission could have decided to address the issue for the entire area through sponsorship of a farmers' market or food bank. Housing and jobs were way out of our depth to tackle systemically, but we could have been a better advocate to the state for improved programs and investments in the community.

As noted in the Preface, the Covid-19 global pandemic and our response to it have highlighted the necessity of assessing and addressing social disparities and risks faced by a large portion of Americans today. Marc Rosen, Director of Healthcare Integration and Translation for the YMCA of the US, has stated in response to this topic, "I think in some ways this (Covid-19) has exacerbated some of the existing dynamics in place around what

I would call a fragmented system for delivering social services to address social needs."[2] Add a dysfunctional solution system to an almost non-existent discovery system, and the problems increase exponentially.

One rare health system in the US that routinely attempts to screen all patients for Social Risks is Promedica in Toledo, Ohio. Before the pandemic, they had instituted a method for screening for patients' social needs, including food insecurity and housing instability. They leveraged this information into some initiatives aimed at food and housing issues, as well as direct investments in the revitalization of local economically distressed neighborhoods. When the pandemic struck and it was obvious that the risks of poor outcomes were based somewhat on social risks and disparities, Promedica already had the wherewithal to identify patients at risk and intervene, as well as be ready to absorb the thousands more placed in Social Risk categories through the economic impact of lost jobs. This head start served their community well during a difficult time.[3]

From a Behavioral Risk perspective, effective information campaigns about smoking cessation, pool safety, or helmet use can easily and cost-effectively be spread by a health system across a larger population and have a positive impact. Such campaigns can be led by Health Systems or in partnership with other medical- or non-medical organizations.

Success depends on knowing what you're addressing and adjusting your strategy appropriately.

Behavioral Health Risks are a quandary in and unto themselves, just as important as the others, or even more so. However, a very different strategy is needed to address these risks. The strategies to address them are similar to those for Behavioral Risks in that one needs both individual resources (like mental health providers and proven clinical pathways of care) as well as widespread community education (especially around recognition and stigma), but the resources and costs are quite different. We'll dig into behavioral health in primary care later in the book.

Population Health, as mentioned earlier, is about improving the health of a population, one patient at a time. For the individual, we need to recognize, uncover, and help them deal with the social risks affecting their health and lives. These efforts may lead to larger initiatives, platforms, and processes to address similar situations across a wide swath of patients; however, it starts with recognizing the needs of the individual patient first.

Acknowledging the individual has long been a challenge in medicine. Sir William Osler, a late nineteenth-century physician often described as the father of modern medicine and a pioneer in medical education, once said that physicians should "care more particularly for the individual patient than for the special features of the disease."[4] In the early twentieth century, writer and physician William Carlos Williams observed how the people that come to see a physician are not merely hearts or livers or kidneys; they are one person with a unique problem.[5] More recently, Stanford medical educator Abraham Varghese channeled Osler when he noted, "Disease is easier to recognize than the individual with the disease."[6] Perhaps it is the disease-oriented education that physicians receive which steers to the appreciation of the disease rather than the person.

Recognizing the individual, though, means finding and addressing the obstacles blocking that person's return to optimum health and well-being, whether those obstacles are medical, social, behavioral, or mental. This recognition enables informed, shared decision-making, and the development of the right Plan of Care to promote true healing for that unique individual. However...

Before you can begin to address, you must assess. When faced with a patient struggling to breathe, we assess their physical vital signs and act accordingly—apply oxygen, support their cardiovascular system, etc. Likewise, we need to assess our patients for social and other risks intentionally so that our Plans of Care are informed and targeted to their specific needs.

As we track and measure what we do in these cases, we need to look for patterns that may lead to larger, more broad-reaching efforts.

Physicians should "care more particularly for the individual patient than for the special features of the disease."

- After we have arranged for one-time respite for a caregiver in a single patient's case, and we then find family caregiver isolation in numerous patients of ours, we might consider starting a support group and a formal respite service.
- When our case managers and social workers are spending long hours in the woods, in tent communities, or homeless shelters caring for cancer patients with central lines and feeding tubes or diabetic patients with festering wounds, we need to find and equip a safe place to house these patients while they are cared for and empowered toward self-management.
- When we discover how many patients are missing appointments or failing to pick up medications due

to a lack of reliable transportation, we can build an accessible and reliable transport system (alone or with non-medical partners) and/or a delivery service for pharmacy supplies.

- When we see how much we, as a health system or provider practice, are spending buying medications for patients who can't afford their prescriptions, we can partner with pharmaceutical companies, pharmacies, pharmacy benefit managers, or philanthropic organizations to supply multiple patients more easily. The list goes on....

Make SDoH a Vital Sign when a patient is assessed. Just do it!

At the same time, we need to build out and bridge our resources to help address these risks as we identify them. Every Emergency Department and every hospital bed has a nearby oxygen hookup to accommodate a hypoxic, short of breath patient. Every ED, hospital, and provider office should also have ready resources to assist a patient and deal with issues around reliable transportation, secure and healthy food sources, affordable and safe housing, etc., partnering with the community rather than trying to solve such issues itself. All of those factors can impair our patient's healing and road to optimum health and well-being.

REFERENCES

1 Hugh Alderwick and Laura Gottlieb (2019). "Meanings and Misunderstandings: Social Determinants of a Health Lexicon for Health Care Systems," The Milbank Quarterly, June 2019, vol. 97 (2019): 1–13.

2 Steven Ross Johnson, "Covid-19 Highlights Need to Tackle Lingering Social Needs," Modern Healthcare, June 13, 2020. https://www.modernhealthcare.com/safety-quality/covid-19-highlights-need-tackle-lingering-social-needs?

3 Johnson, "Covid-19 Highlights Need."

4 William Osler, MD. "Address to the students of the Albany Medical College. Albany Medical Annals," Journal of the Alumni Association of the Albany Medical College, vol. 20 (1899): 307–309. Accessed on https://archive.org/details/albanymedicalann2018medi/page/n319/mode/2up

5 Krista Tippett, "How Do You Want to Be When You Grow Up?," On Being podcast with Abraham Varghese and Denise Pope, May 23, 2019.

6 Tippett, "How Do You Want to Be."

An Example of Social Risk Mitigation

——

A FEW YEARS BACK, a health system in the Southeastern region of the US piloted a program to reduce hospital readmissions by delivering healthy meals to patients with malnutrition plus heart failure, COPD/emphysema, or pneumonia after they were discharged from the hospital. By providing these meals to this select group of patients for thirty days post-hospitalization, the health system showed a marked decrease in the readmission rate of these folks. In other words, by identifying a nutritional need in patients and meeting that need, the health system helped improve health and well-being in these patients to the point of allowing them to stay in their homes longer before needing additional "rescue care" from the hospitals.

This program, though obviously successful in improving health and decreasing readmissions, sputtered along for a few years before the health system finally shut it down. The rationale was that the health system couldn't see how to pay or get paid for it. There was no billable charge to generate for the service, and the health system had not yet entered into any value-based, prospective payment programs with any payers. The leaders of the program looked for grant money from payers and other organizations like AARP to keep this program alive, a program they knew had benefit and had proven so. Meanwhile, the health system continued to pay millions of dollars in penalties to Medicare (CMS) for excess readmissions due to rapid decompensation of patients' health proximal to hospital discharge.

A couple of years later, the health system had set up an Accountable Care Organization (ACO) with CMS for its fee for service Medicare patients. The main goals in an ACO, which is accountable for all costs associated with the care of its patients, are to reduce cost of care while maintaining or improving quality delivered to the patient cohort. A large percentage of the potentially avoidable costs for these patients come from admissions and readmissions to the hospital due to exacerbations or worsening of chronic medical problems and acute infections, like pneumonia, and skin or kidney infections (usually in people with comorbid chronic medical conditions).

In other words, the cost of care is most significantly and negatively affected when patients with chronic medical conditions decompensate either due to poor control of their condition(s) or due to external forces, such as malnourishment, inability to follow up with medical care or to fill prescriptions, and abrupt change in their housing or environmental situation, etc. Obviously, the best way to avoid readmission is to avoid admission in the first place, so ideal chronic disease management and mitigation of external forces could aid in health and well-being optimization, thereby preventing admission or readmission to the hospital.

With this in mind, the ACO, which already had a care management program designed to guide patients to improved self-management of their risks and chronic conditions, took a look at applying the delivered meals program to its patients. Following the principle of Risk Stratification to identify the patients most in need and potentially most benefitted by the program, the ACO decided to pilot a meal delivery program to a very specific cohort of patients–those living at home with the diagnoses of malnutrition and COPD and heart failure. It is no surprise that this group of patients was the source of numerous Emergency Department (ED) visits, hospitalizations, and readmissions, accounting for almost six times the cost of care compared to the average ACO patient.

The plan was to identify these patients, engage them in the delivered meals program for three to four months, and then measure the changes seen in healthcare utilization of these patients. If they were not already enrolled in the care management programs of the ACO, they were also placed in such a program.

Of the patients who met the criteria, some declined the program, either initially due to not wanting "strangers in the house" or after a few meals due to not liking the meal choices. For those who continued in the program, though, the benefits were tremendous. For the fifteen or so patients who participated over four months, ED use was cut by almost 80 percent and inpatient admissions were cut by 100 percent—meaning that in this group of patients who previously each averaged almost an admission per month, there were no admissions in four months—zero!

In addition to enjoying improved health and staying at home (rather than at a hospital), the cost of care for this small group of fifteen would save the ACO $600,000 per year. While the patients were also enrolled in the ACO's care management programs, the benefits of this meal delivery program far outweighed the benefits that the care management programs offered alone. Obviously, this was a very high-risk cohort, but the benefits to the patients and the ACO were huge! The next step for the ACO was to broaden the field of patients at risk to see how much impact could be made on the group of next lower risk.

As well as meeting the nutritional needs of the patients, there was a social aspect to the program. Along with the care management support, a social worker checked in by phone with each patient weekly. There was also benefit from the patients' perspectives of having a human deliver the meals once a week and engage in some conversation. These collateral benefits made the meal delivery program even more effective at addressing other social risks–in this case, the risk associated with social isolation.

How Not to Evaluate Social Risks

———

AN ESSENTIAL ELEMENT IN the successful assessment and addressing of Social Risks is the focus on the individual. Certainly, just as it's good to understand the prevalence of diabetes or hypertension in a cohort of patients in order to know where one's care focus may need to be directed, knowing the social risk tendencies of a group of patients based on geography, payer, age, or another parameter can help discern generally where to look for problems and direct mitigating initiatives. However, if the data collection and analysis stops there, with the group, much of the value to the individual will be lost.

In the course of building numerous value-based lines of business, I've entertained the sales pitches of multiple vendors trying to sell their wares to help us better serve our populations. One company in particular stands out in my mind as we consider the use of data to address the Social Risks of an individual.

This company stated that, through the analysis of numerous databases they had purchased, they could drill down into each zip code and build a list of all the potential Social Risks that are present in that area and the statistical probability that someone in that zip code has a particular risk factor. Their pitch was that this information would be useful not only to know what mitigation programs to focus on for those geographic areas but also would prompt the provider to ask specific questions pertaining to those particular risks when conversing with the patient.

The problems with this approach, as we pointed out to the vendor, were threefold. First of all, a propensity toward a specific risk does not mean the risk exists, so the provider still needs to inquire about social risks with the patient. The provider should be doing this with every patient anyway.

Second, most providers seeing patients in a specific area could likely give an impromptu analysis of social risks by zip code. Physicians and (particularly) their staff members are generally sufficiently familiar with the areas they serve to know that patients in one area are prone to food or housing insecurity whereas others living elsewhere are not. That fairly high level of knowledge and insight is likely just as accurate when done with pen or pencil off the top of an insightful provider's head compared to a detailed analysis of multiple purchased databases.

Yet in my opinion the third issue is the most important. If the company's goal is to guide provider questioning of their patients based on the likelihood of certain risks in their area, the distinct possibility exists that Social Risks in a patient living outside the "typical" area will be missed. Though more prevalent in one zip code or block-level analysis, all adverse SDoH that affect a patient's health can exist in any neighborhood. It would be unfortunate for me not to ask about, and thereby miss an opportunity to assist with, food insecurity, social isolation, transportation issues, interpersonal violence, or lack of connectivity just because of someone's zip code.

Certainly, zip code data, or better yet, block-level data of potential Social Risks can inform a provider or health system of the highest propensity issues that they may need to mitigate. That fits in with the building of processes–broad and general programs available to deploy. But, as noted numerous times, a Plan of Care, a patient-specific plan, needs to be based completely on the needs of that individual patient. The only way to assess the needs of that individual is to ask them directly.

CHAPTER FIVE

Behavioral Health (BH) in Primary Care

BEHAVIORAL AND MENTAL HEALTH play a fundamental role in the optimization of one's health and well-being. For years we have separated mental health from physical health, and we are just starting to re-acknowledge the vital position of our psychological health in our overall well-being. Because of this split between physical and mental health, primary care physicians and providers (as well as all other non-mental health professionals) have shied away from assessing and addressing psychological and psychiatric conditions, to the detriment of their patients' overall health.

This chapter is in no way meant to be an all-inclusive, end-all discourse on the diagnosis and treatment of Behavioral and Mental Health (BHMH) conditions in primary care medicine. Rather, it is intended to serve as a source of foundational information and ideas, highlighting the importance of incorporating screening and treatment for common BHMH conditions. From there, a primary care provider (PCP) can dive deeper into the topic and augment the care of patients in their practice. I touch mainly on why screening is an important topic, and encouragement to consider making screening routine with some brief attention to basic treatment into the PCP setting, with or without an integrated BHMH professional in the practice. I urge providers and practice managers to do the work of figuring out how they can best meet the needs of their patients.

Therefore, this is not so much a look at "how to" identify and care for BHMH conditions as it is a look into "why" should we care. This chapter is a bit more clinical and granular in data than the rest of the book but bear with me; there's a big payoff.

Why should we be so concerned about this topic? According to the World Health Organization, Major Depressive Disorder is the leading cause of disability among Americans age 15 to 44.[1] Beyond that, depression and anxiety account for very common comorbidities in patients with chronic medical conditions, comorbidities that both exacerbate those chronic medical conditions and are worsened by them.[2] To make matters worse, a large proportion of these affected patients do not even seek treatment.

Below are examples of this disparity in depressed adolescent and adult patients:

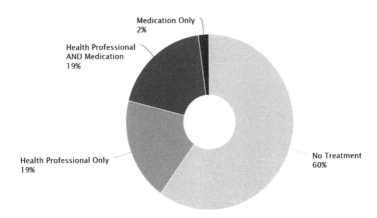

Past Year Treatment Received Among Adolescents with Major Depressive Episode (2016)

Data Courtesy of SAMHSA

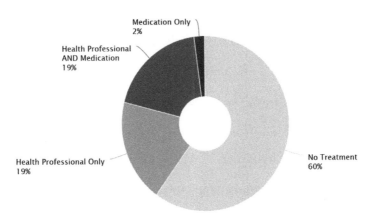

Past Year Treatment Received Among Adolescents with Major Depressive Episode (2016)

Data Courtesy of SAMHSA

Factors contributing to this lack of treatment include societal stigma toward mental health, a relative shortage of BHMH professionals throughout much of the US, and the hesitancy of non-psychiatric physicians and providers to screen for and/or treat BHMH conditions in their practices.

The economic burden of BHMH conditions is staggering. For Major Depression alone, over $200 billion is spent annually to treat depressive disorders, with depressive disorders being the sixth-most costly health condition overall. Forty-five percent of these costs were attributable to the costs of all healthcare

The majority of the costs related to depression are due to treatments and complications of comorbid medical conditions.

treatment, 5 percent to suicide-related costs, and 50 percent to workplace costs, with only 38 percent of the total costs being directly due to Major Depression itself. The majority of the costs were due to treatments and complications of comorbid medical conditions (like cardiovascular disease, cerebrovascular disease, diabetes, cancer, etc.)[3], which account for the largest portion of the growing economic burden of Major Depression.

Up to one in four primary care patients suffer from depression; yet, primary care doctors identify less than one-third (31 percent) of these patients. In other words, instead of identifying BHMH conditions in 25 percent of their patients, as expected, physicians are only identifying about 8 percent of their patients as having BHMH conditions. This is no surprise considering the low rate at which PCPs screen their patients for depression. According to a survey of almost a million office visits in 2015, depression screening was documented as occurring only 4.4 percent of the time, whereas height, weight, and blood pressure were documented 70.5 percent, 76.1 percent, and 68.4 percent of the time, respectively. Even retinal and eye exams, an area many primary care physicians claim to feel inadequate in examining and treating, were performed over 15 percent of the time.[4]

Granted, since that survey in 2015, more electronic medical records (EMR) have added quick and easy ways to screen for and document depression and anxiety, but in reality the number of screenings has not increased appreciably except where providers are incentivized to meet certain screening numbers in value-based contracts they have with payers. While the valuable and validated screening tools of PHQ-2 and PHQ-9 (two questions or nine questions) are built into many EMRs now, providers just need to use them. A PHQ-9 score greater than 10 has a sensitivity of 88 percent and a specificity of 88 percent for Major Depressive

Disorder, and the reliability and validity of the tool have indicated it has sound psychometric properties.[5] In short, these are proven and necessary tools for PCPs to use.

Another useful yes-no questionnaire is the Columbia-Suicide Severity Rating Scale. Using this tool can stratify patients in real-time as to who needs immediate, complex, high-level intervention now versus those who can be managed more deliberately, and this knowledge can save lives.

To be clear, I am not suggesting that all psychiatric cases can or should be diagnosed and treated in the PCP setting. Certainly, conditions like bipolar disorder, schizophrenia, and other severe mental illnesses need to be managed primarily by psychiatrists or other mental health professionals. Yet PCPs manage hypertension, diabetes, heart failure, arthritis, and other conditions without the primary use of a sub-specialist, referring patients with complicated cases or when surgical procedures are necessary. The same can hold true in the BHMH realm, especially for conditions like depression and anxiety.

The biggest problem is that PCPs aren't even screening patients to identify these conditions. The physicians to whom I've spoken who don't screen do so because they say they have no resources for the patient should they screen positive. They aren't comfortable or are not interested in caring for depression or anxiety, and it can take months to get a patient in to see a BHMH professional. The problem with this approach is that it waits for patients to reach a crisis (like a suicide attempt) before they can access care through the Emergency Department via an involuntary hold. This is a horribly inefficient and ineffective (and expensive!) way to treat any chronic condition, but especially depression or anxiety. Failure to screen for depression and anxiety prevents us both from seeing the prevalence of these conditions in a community and from assessing the adequacy of resources available to meet the needs.

We would not take this unproductive and hopeless approach in the treatment of any other healthcare issue. Failing to screen for depression does not mean that it doesn't exist and that it's not wreaking havoc on the patient's health and well-being. Failing to screen for colon or breast cancer simply because there's no easy access to an oncologic surgeon would not be tolerated and would be considered negligent on the part of the provider. To do so would mean we just wait for the patient to present in crisis, and at that point we may not be able to render much help.

Failing to screen for depression does not mean that it doesn't exist and that it's not wreaking havoc on the patient's health and well-being.

Meanwhile, the surreptitious presence of BHMH conditions

like depression and anxiety, until addressed, is actively compromising the treatment of patients with chronic medical conditions, just as the unidentified cancer continues to destroy the healthy tissue around it while it awaits discovery.

Let's reconsider the patients with chronic medical problems and the influence that BHMH conditions like depression and anxiety exert on them. A health system with which I once worked with was so fixated on thirty-day readmissions that I was required to express any project or initiative in terms of its positive impact on readmissions. Therefore, I've got some facts and figures to show the significant impact of BHMH conditions on "medical" health issues, which I uncovered in the process of trying to justify having social workers on the medical floors of the system's hospitals. These social workers would address both Social Risks as well as screen for and address BHMH conditions (in conjunction with the hospitalists and outpatient BHMH professionals).

As noted above, about 25 percent of the population has a mental health condition. Of those, 68 percent have medical issues of one kind or another. The coincidence of depression in heart failure (HF) is 40 percent, in COPD 35 percent, in acute myocardial infarction (AMI) 25 percent, in diabetes, 35 percent, and in pneumonia 20 percent, to name a few of the most common conditions landing someone in the hospital. For the same conditions, the prevalence of anxiety is about 20, 20, 20, 25, and 10 percent, respectively.[6]

The overall thirty-day readmission (ReAd) rate for patients with the chronic conditions of HF, pneumonia, and AMI is over 500 basis points higher when comorbid MH condition present (21.7 percent vs. 16.5 percent).[7] Split out by specific comorbid conditions:

Risk of ReAd with HF + Depression = 1.5x

Risk of ReAd with COPD + Depression = 2x

Risk of ReAd with COPD + Anxiety = 1.4x

AMI ReAd with BHMH diagnosis = 12.1 percent vs. 9.2 percent without

Pneumonia ReAd with BHMH diagnosis = 20.2 percent vs. 16.2 percent without[8]

Applying these numbers to the readmissions of this particular health system in one year, for the primary conditions of heart failure, COPD, AMI, and pneumonia, over 75 percent of the patients readmitted within thirty days of discharge would have had a BHMH comorbidity of depression or anxiety, with heart failure and COPD comorbidities accounting for 86 percent and 98 percent, respectively. These BHMH comorbidities, based on the medical literature, were exerting a tremendous negative force on these patients thought to be afflicted only with "medical" conditions.

Consider that for a minute. The frequency of depression and/or anxiety in these patients is significantly higher than the general population, as is the risk of readmission associated with the comorbid presence of depression and anxiety. If the BHMH comorbidities of depression and anxiety go unidentified and untreated in this cohort, these patients will fail their Plan of Care and land back in the hospital at a high rate, regardless of stellar medical treatment following all of their non-BHMH recommendations for the standard of care clinical pathways to treat their medical conditions. We're setting up the patients for failure by not assessing and addressing BHMH conditions.

Addressing their depression and anxiety, though, can have a significant positive impact on their outcomes.

In the table on the following page, the Current ReAd Rate represents the percent readmission into the health system in theprior year for each condition and then the overall rate for all causes at the bottom. The 100 percent column denotes what the Readmission Rate could be if the BHMH comorbidities were perfectly identified and controlled, including the impact on All Causes. The 25 percent, likewise, reflects the effect on readmissions

	Current ReAd Rate	100%	25%	50%	70%	80%
HF	24.60%	3.44%	19.31%	14.02%	9.79%	7.68%
COPD	24.84%	0.49%	18.75%	12.67%	7.80%	5.36%
AMI	15.84%	6.57%	13.52%	11.21%	9.35%	8.43%
PNA	18.22%	11.11%	16.44%	14.67%	13.24%	12.53%
All Causes	16.67%	13.82%	15.96%	15.24%	14.67%	14.39%

if only a quarter of the patients were screened and appropriately treated for conditions of depression and anxiety. That 25 percent improvement column may not seem particularly noteworthy, but for this specific system such an improvement would add a tremendously important Quality Star to their governmental CMS Star rating! Moving the needle by finding and appropriately addressing just 25 percent of the BHMH comorbid conditions would save this health system millions of dollars in CMS readmission penalties...and oh, by the way, since every percentage point represents a person and the lives around that person, there would be a significant positive impact on the health and well-being of many people, the patients plus their families and broader work and social communities.

Looking specifically at HF patients, when major depression coexists with HF, there are adverse prognostic implications in patients hospitalized for heart failure.[9] A different metanalysis showed that depression and HF share pathophysiological mechanisms and that the adverse effects of depression on the outcomes in HF to include reduced quality of life, reduced preventive healthcare use, increased re-hospitalization, and increased mortality. In fact, there is a twofold increase in mortality in HF patients with Depression compared to those without.[10]

Let's consider an even more common condition and one that is also a major contributor to HF–hypertension (HTN). According to the CDC, from 2015 to 2016 the prevalence of HTN was 29 percent in the US population, and it increases with age: age group 18–39, 7.5 percent; 40–59, 33.2 percent; and 60 and over, 63.1 percent.[11] According to the medical literature, depression affects approximately one-third of hypertensive patients,[12] and depression or its symptoms can interfere with blood pressure control.[13] Furthermore, a randomized controlled trial integrating depression and HTN treatment showed success in improving patient outcomes.[14]

The effects on COPD are no different. About 40 percent of COPD patients have severe depressive symptoms or clinical depression, and data suggest that co-morbid depression may be an independent predictor for mortality.[15]

By this point it should be obvious that depression and

anxiety, the two most common BHMH conditions, and ones that generally can be treated in the primary care setting, frequently coexist with the chronic medical problems that bring people in to see a doctor, and that failing to identify and treat depression or anxiety will limit the effectiveness of treatment for these other chronic medical conditions. The result is a patient who does not enjoy optimal health and well-being, who is more likely to end up in the hospital, and who will likely fail a Plan of Care, landing back in the hospital for readmission in short order. All the while, their care is costing more and more healthcare dollars without the desired positive outcomes.

Hopefully, the above information has persuaded you of the value of screening at least for depression and anxiety in the primary care setting. The next question that docs always throw out is: "I've found a patient with depression. Now what?" If you find yourself in an area where it's next to impossible to get a patient into a BHMH professional due to availability or financial considerations, there are some potential solutions out there.

Ideally, patients identified with depression and/or anxiety in the primary care setting would be treated by a mental health professional integrated into the PCP's office. The BHMH Professional shares space, patients, and communication channels with the PCPs in the office, and often a patient who screens positive for depression or anxiety can be introduced to the BHMH Professional that same day and get a treatment plan lined up.

Time and again the medical literature has shown this integrated model to be very successful. Practices engaged in Value-based Care have embraced it, whether such practices are paid prospectively to maintain and improve patients' health or are given retrospective incentives for quality and outcomes. In fact, practices that have embraced value in this way find they cannot stop practicing within this model. They see the obstacles to improved outcomes for their patients if they leave BHMH issues unaddressed, and they choose to overcome those obstacles for their patients.

If your practice has not yet made the leap to value, or you struggle to get patients seen by MHBH professionals, at least two other options exist: Digital Cognitive Behavioral Therapy (DCBT) and BHMH Telemedicine/Telepsychiatry. Both of these options effectively increase the BHMH network of providers available to a practitioner.

For almost two decades now, the United Kingdom's National Health System has effectively used DCBT for its citizens. Patient-guided DCBT with appropriate support from care managers has proven as effective as face-to-face CBT for the treatment of many conditions, including mild to moderate depression and anxiety. By employing this strategy on primary care patients in the United States who have been screened and shown to have mild or moderate depression and/or anxiety, PCPs could get their patients on to the right track to treat adequately and appropriately both the BHMH conditions and the patients' chronic medical problems.

The use of DCBT could either serve as a bridge while waiting to access a face-to-face visit with a BHMH professional or as actual treatment of the patient's condition, with or without the addition of medication. Either way, the network of available BHMH providers would be effectively increased by decreasing the demand or urgency of an appointment for low to moderate severity patients or eliminating the need altogether.

It's more obvious how BHMH Telemedicine, or what we refer to as Telepsych, would increase the available network of providers. I started working on Telemedicine solutions with a health system back in the late 1990s, and mental health visits were one of the easier circumstances to solve. Since then, numerous insurance payers have been covering Telepysch services for the evaluation and follow-up of patients with documented BHMH conditions, like depression and anxiety.

If a primary care provider deploys the basic infrastructure for a video Telemedicine visit in their office, it's not too difficult to get a patient set up with a BHMH provider while they're still in the office. Continued consultations can occur back in the PCP's office, or via a computer or smart device owned by the patient. Either way, the effectiveness of this type of management for mild to moderate depression and anxiety is well-documented as safe and effective. A robust program from the PCP's office to manage a patient's care adds to the effectiveness of this approach. As with DCBT, referral through Telepsych increases the availability of face-to-face services for more severe, at-risk patients by having those of lesser severity seek care through an alternative path.

While physicians and providers may think they can focus solely on the chronic "medical" issues of their patients and ignore the BHMH issues they're facing, the above information should dispel such notions. The data is pretty clear: simply prescribing treatment to the organ-specific domain of a chronic disease will likely be less than optimal due to the frequent coexistence of BHMH conditions that actively worsen those medical conditions. As with Social Risks, though, in order to address, you must first assess.

The data is pretty clear: simply prescribing treatment to the organ-specific domain of a chronic disease will likely be less than optimal due to the frequent coexistence of BHMH conditions that actively worsen those medical conditions.

Screening for and then arranging treatment for comorbid depression and anxiety will render the medical prescriptions much more effective. This leads to improved health and well-being for our patients exemplified in decreased hospital admissions and readmissions, thus improving both the quality and the experience. Of course, cost is lessened and optimized in this setting as well, creating enormous value for the patient and the system.

REFERENCES

1 https://report.nih.gov/NIHfactsheets/ViewFactsheet. aspx?csid=48

2 B. Sutor , T. A. Rummans, S. G. Jowsey, L. E. Krahn, M. J. Martin, M. K. O'Connor, K. L. Philbrick, and J. W. Richardson, "Major depression in medically ill patients," Mayo Clin Proc., vol. 73 no.4 (April 1998):329–337.

3 P.E. Greenberg, The Journal of Clinical Psychiatry, vol. 76, no. 2 (Feb 2015): 155–162.

4 NCHS, National Ambulatory Medical Care Survey, 2015.

5 K. Kroenke, R.L. Spitzer, & J. B. Williams, "The PHQ-9: validity of a brief depression severity measure," Journal of General Internal Medicine, vol. 16, no. 9 (2001): 606–613.

6 E. Andreoulakis, T. Hyphantis, D. Kandylis, and A. Iacovides, "Depression in Diabetes Mellitus: A Comprehensive Review," Hippokratia, vol. 16, no. 3 (July–Sept 2012): 205–214.

Hsin-Pei Feng, RN, PhD, et al., "Risk of Anxiety and Depressive Disorders in Patients with Myocardial Infarction: A Nationwide Population-based Cohort Study," Medicine (Baltimore) vol. 95, no. 34 (Aug 2016): e4464.

Kenneth E. Freedland, PhD; Robert M. Carney, PhD; and Michael W. Rich, MD, "Impact of Depression on Prognosis in Heart Failure," Heart Failure Clinics, vol. 7, no. 1 (Jan 2011): 11–21.

Anand S. Iye, et al., "Depression Is Associated with Readmission for Acute Exacerbation of Chronic Obstructive Pulmonary

Disease," Annals of the American Thoracic Society, vol. 13, no. 2 (Feb 2016): 197–203.

Rajesh Rajput et al., "Prevalence and Predictors of Depression and Anxiety in Patients of Diabetes Mellitus in a Tertiary Care Center," Indian Journal of Endocrinology and Metabolism, vol. 20, no. 6 (Nov–Dec 2016: 746–751.

Gurinder Singh, MD, et al., "Association of Psychological Disorders With 30-Day Readmission Rates in Patients With COPD," CHEST vol. 149 no. 4 (2016): 905–915.

Kim Germaine Smolderen, Ph.D., "Coping After an Acute Myocardial Infarction: The Role of Depression and Anxiety," American College of Cardiology (Jan 04, 2017).

Brett Thombs, Ph.D., et al., "Prevalence of Depression in Survivors of Acute Myocardial Infarction: Review of the Evidence," Journal of General Internal Medicine, vol. 21 no. 1 (Jan 2006): 30–38.

7 Brian K. Ahmedani, Ph.D., M.S., et al., "Influence of psychiatric comorbidity on 30-day readmissions for heart failure, myocardial infarction, and pneumonia." Psychiatry Service, vol. 66 no.2 (Feb 2015): 134–140.

Linda Calvillo–King, et al., "Impact of Social Factors on Risk of Readmission or Mortality in Pneumonia and Heart Failure: Systematic Review," Journal of General Internal Medicine vol. 28, no. 2 (February 2013): 269–282.

8 Brian K. Ahmedani, Ph.D., M.S., et al., "Influence of psychiatric comorbidity on 30-day readmissions for heart failure, myocardial infarction, and pneumonia." Psychiatry Service, vol. 66 no. 2 (Feb 1, 2015): 134–140.

Linda Calvillo-King, et al., "Impact of Social Factors on Risk of Readmission or Mortality in Pneumonia and Heart Failure: Systematic Review." Journal of General Internal Medicine, vol. 28, no. 2 (February 2013): 269–282.

Kenneth E. Freedland, Ph.D., et al., "Depression and Multiple Rehospitalizations in Patients With Heart Failure," Clinical Cardiology, vol. 39, no. 5 (2016): 257–262.

Kenneth E. Freedland, Ph.D.; Robert M. Carney, PhD; and Michael W. Rich, M.D., "Impact of Depression on Prognosis in Heart Failure," Heart Failure Clinics, vol. 7, no. 1 (Jan 1, 2011): 11–21.

Anand S. Iye, et al., "Depression Is Associated with Readmission for Acute Exacerbation of Chronic Obstructive Pulmonary Disease," Annals of the American Thoracic Society, vol. 13, no. 2 (Feb 2016): 197–203.

Gurinder Singh, M.D., et al., "Association of Psychological Disorders With 30-Day Readmission Rates in Patients With COPD," CHEST vol. 149, no. 4 (2016): 905–915.

Smolderen, Kim Germaine PhD. "Coping After an Acute Myocardial Infarction: The Role of Depression and Anxiety," American College of Cardiology, Jan 04, 2017.

9 K.E. Freedland, R.M. Carney, M.W. Rich, A. Caracciolo, J.A. Krotenberg, L.I. Smith, et al., "Depression in Elderly Patients with Congestive Heart Failure," Journal of Geriatric Psychiatry vol. 24 (1991): 59–71.

10 Amam Mbakwem, Francis Aina, and Casmir Amadi, "Expert Opinion—Depression in Patients with Heart Failure: Is

Enough Being Done?" Cardiac Failure Review, vol. 2, no. 2 (Nov. 2016): 110–112.

11 https://www.cdc.gov/nchs/products/databriefs/db289.htm

12 Z. Li, Y. Li, L. Chen, P. Chen, Y. Hu, "Prevalence of Depression in Patients with Hypertension: A Systematic Review and Meta-Analysis," Medicine (Baltimore) vol. 94 no. 31 (2015): e1317.

13 A. F. Rubio-Guerra, L. Rodriguez-Lopez, G. Vargas-Ayala, S. Huerta-Ramirez, D.C. Serna, and J. J. Lozano-Nuevo, "Depression Increases the Risk for Uncontrolled Hypertension," Experimental & Clinical Cardiology, vol. 18, no.1 (2013): 10–12.

14 H.R. Bogner and H.F. de Vries, "Integration of Depression and Hypertension Treatment: A Pilot, Randomized Controlled Trial." Annals of Family Medicine, vol. 6 no. 4 (2008): 295–301.

15 K. B. Stage, T. Middelboe, T.B. Stage, et al., "Depression in COPD-management and Quality of Life Considerations," International Journal of Chronic Obstructive Pulmonary Disease, vol. 1 (2006): 315–320.

Gurinder Singh, M.D., et al., "Association of Psychological Disorders With 30-Day Readmission Rates in Patients With COPD," CHEST vol. 149, no, 4 (2016):905–915.

———

CHAPTER SIX

Reframing: A Positive, Patient-centered Perspective

FOR YEARS, HOSPITALS AND HEALTH systems have been trying (with varying success) to lower their readmission rates—the percent of people discharged from the hospital who then readmit back to the hospital within thirty days of their discharge. Much of the attention over the past few years has been paid because these facilities have started to owe penalty dollars to CMS/Medicare (and now some commercial payers) if their readmission rate is over a certain percent. Because these penalties can amount to millions of dollars for a health system, so there is a financial motivation to fix this issue.

It's a bit disheartening that simply the knowledge of patients landing back in the hospital so soon after discharge was insufficient to get providers and facilities to see readmissions as a priority. The days of volume-based care apparently were quite proficient at encouraging folks to turn a blind eye to people who kept returning to the hospital. They'd just "rescue" them again and drop another bill (cha-ching!). Yet a focus on value, rather than volume, brings this issue to the forefront because readmission likely reflects decreased quality, increased cost, and worse patient experience—all directional changes in the Value Equation that lower the value proposition.

I believe that the vast majority of readmissions within a month of discharge occur because we, as providers and facilities, fail in our delivery of care, either in quality or coordination. A failure in quality could refer to prescribing the wrong treatment or the wrong Plan of Care for that patient's individual conditions and needs. A failure in coordination—probably the more common issue—represents a breakdown in the communication and management of the devised Plan of Care, leading to a lack of Longitudinal Support through all the transitions of the healthcare journey. Certainly, some patients are so fragile that they are "hospital-dependent," but those folks likely represent the minority of readmitted patients at this time. Currently what we as healthcare providers do or don't do leads to the majority of readmissions.

More importantly, the reality is that the patient is penalized more for readmission than is the facility. Their health and well-being were not optimized to the point of keeping them out of the hospital shortly after already being there. Clearly, most patients and families don't want their health to worsen to the point of needing another trip to the hospital soon after leaving.

I would love to start a campaign to reframe how we view someone's journey and disposition after leaving a hospital. Perhaps if we reframe how we think about readmissions, we might have a more positive impact.

The 30-day All-Cause Readmission Rate is a facility-centric measure of failure.

As it stands, the 30-day All-Cause Readmission Rate is a *facility-centric measure of failure*. To have a real impact, we may need to change our perspective to a *patient-centric, positive measure*, such as **Home Success Rate**. This change in perspective could accomplish the following:

- Put the focus back on the patient, where it belongs
- Give healthcare providers a positive goal for which to strive
- Emphasize that every patient's journey home is unique

Let's look at each of these accomplishments individually.

Patient-Centric

We all talk about keeping the patient in the "center" of the health-care model and numerous examples and analogies accentuate this point. As an aside, there are times a "patient in the center" analogy is not necessarily a good thing. For instance, consider a vision of an organizational campfire. Don't put the patient in the middle! … Or a dinner table–obviously. I've worked with organizations where they let that analogy get a bit out of hand.

This health system, in devising their process for strategy development and deployment, produced a very elegant baseball diamond analogy for planning, communicating, implementing, and checking their strategic plan. It was a beautiful metaphorical image of the process, showing each of the steps as the bases were rounded. Then, someone thought that to make it patient-centric they should put the patient on the pitcher's mound, in the middle of the picture. That ruined it, for me at least. In that representation, the patient was now the defensive adversary of the health system, who was at the plate hitting the balls pitched and running the bases. Instead of placing on the mound the external forces like regulations, legislation, payers, etc. that actually throw curve-balls to health systems, they placed the patient squarely on the opposing team.

Without me exposing too much of my pedantic nature, suffice

it to say that the best models, images, and analogies either stick to the intended message or stop when the analogy is stretched too thin. Language and images are too influential on our thinking and perspectives to ignore this. In any case, let's picture the patient in the center simply as a way to focus our efforts in support of the patient.

The Triple Aim of CMS encourages the following: improving the individual experience of care, improving the health of populations, and reducing the per capita costs of care for populations. All of these goals are patient-centric, and they represent improving the health of the population as the primary goal, with two contributory secondary goals: improving patient experience and reducing costs. The addition of the fourth aim–improving the work-life of clinicians and staff–has emphasized that providers and staff need to feel joy and accomplishment in performing their roles of health care. (In other words, they, too, need to feel valued!) The fourth aim is provider-centric but also recognizes that the only way to keep the patient as the focal point is to have engaged, satisfied providers to guide patients on their journeys.

Success in other quality metrics like catheter or central line infections (CAUTI and CLABSI) has been achieved at a higher rate in facilities where the individual patients and their needs are emphasized over a focus on the silicone or plastic tubes that we've inserted into their bodies. Safety and quality in operating rooms increases when not only a safety "Time Out" is taken preoperatively to verify the site of surgery and patient identity, but also when the patient's story of who they are, what family they have, and their goals of having the surgery is shared out loud before the surgical team begins work.

Humanization of a process through an intentional effort to focus on the patient and their unique circumstances leads to success.

Humanization of a process in this way, through an intentional effort to focus on the patient and their unique circumstances, leads to success. As with Social Risks, you can't address what you don't assess. Until the humanity of the patient is recognized and assessed, healthcare providers cannot address the needs of the individual, and therefore cannot create value instead of widgets.

Such is the focus of reframing readmissions. Concentrating on the success of optimizing a patient's health long enough for them to stay at home for a significant period of time emphasizes the humanity of the patient. This redirection of the focus of readmissions from the number of times a patient returns to our turf to how often the patient remains on theirs emphasizes the patient's journey, not ours. Such a reframing can aid us in resetting the priorities to achieve that goal.

A Positive Goal for Providers

Striving for a positive outcome is generally more appealing and often a more powerful motivator than avoidance of a negative one. Think about that in terms of your own day-to-day living, and you'll see the wisdom. We all do much better in our jobs when we actively strive for a positive goal rather than working not to get fired. Focusing on how to reach a positive outcome for the organization will always lead to a better outcome than concentrating on not making one's boss mad. Our personal relationships work out better when we intentionally strive to make others feel loved than when we just try to avoid them leaving the relationship. Sometimes the actions required to gain the positive are the same as to avoid the negative, but the motivation can make all the difference.

Sometimes the actions required to gain the positive are the same as to avoid the negative, but the motivation can make all the difference.

Of course, the threat of pain and suffering can be a substantial motivator to the primitive portions of our brains, but positive rewards (and their accompanying Dopamine release) are even more powerful motivators, including the incentive for us to find new and creative ways to overcome or avoid potential pain and suffering in order to achieve a desired positive outcome. Framing the problem of readmissions (or patient care, in general) in terms of patient success may open our minds to new and elastic thinking that helps us find ways to achieve that goal while avoiding the associated pain and pitfalls.

Additionally, framing in a positive light can aid in our storytelling being used as a tool to galvanize processes and goals; storytelling is a powerful and under-utilized tool for motivating and building culture. We will always need to investigate the negative stories in a root cause analysis, and sometimes these need to be shared with the team. Yet consider how motivating it could be to share success stories of patients with challenging situations overcome through the proper application of quality and coordination (risk stratification, plan of care, and longitudinal support). Looking at a Home Success Rate story, noting where issues were anticipated, difficulties in communication and coordination were overcome, and where a patient's potentially rough transitions were proactively and intentionally smoothed, can instill the desired focus for providers, highlight the joy of serving medically, and stimulate a continuation of the successful processes.

Every Patient is Unique

There's a reason hospitals and health systems aren't usually successful in moving the readmissions needle by merely instituting one or two initiatives aimed at decreasing readmissions. Every patient's journey is different, and has diverse challenges and twists and turns in the road. A single roadmap for discharge or even a limited menu of services and programs will not meet the needs of every patient.

Reframing readmission avoidance (or: How do we keep the patient from needing to come back to the hospital?) into how we can help the patient to return and stay in their chosen home, changes our perspective. We know quite well the paths and doors that lead to our facilities, but do we know the doors and paths that lead to the patient's unique home setting and all the obstacles and pitfalls along the way? Not intuitively, we don't. But through active, intentional engagement with the patient and family we can better understand their unique circumstances and discern ways over, around, or through their obstacles.

> *We know quite well the paths and doors that lead to our facilities, but do we know the doors and paths that lead to the patient's unique home setting and all the obstacles and pitfalls along the way?*

Again: Processes should be broad and standardized, but plans must be specific and individualized. Social Determinants of Health should be assessed like a patient's vital signs so that the unique risks for that person can be identified and mitigated.

Consider an auto repair shop. The mechanics and body shop workers assume that when the vehicle is ready to leave the shop, the driver will come and pick up the vehicle and is equipped with the knowledge and wherewithal to leave the shop and go about their business. They trust that the driver will pay attention to the dashboard's signs and alerts and that the driver is licensed and capable of operating the vehicle safely.

In healthcare, we often assume the same things about our patients. When they're ready for discharge from the hospital to home, we assume that they are unhindered and fully able to resume their appropriate activities.

There are knowledgeable, proficient, and well-resourced drivers who have accidents or whose vehicles have simply worn to the point of needing major service. These people tend to leave the shop and do just fine. Reminding them to get an oil change after they leave, or even scheduling it for them, and making a follow-up phone call to them two to three days after they leave, will help ensure their success. However, if we only build processes to focus on keeping these people out of the shop soon after they leave, we'll miss many of the issues that bring the bulk of the others back soon after leaving.

What about the person who's unsure of how to operate their car? Soon after they leave the shop, such people tend to land in a ditch or run into something, necessitating a return visit. Then there are people who either ignore or don't understand the dashboard warning lights signaling an issue in need of being addressed. What if the person repeatedly leaves the shop without enough money to refill their fuel tank, and every time it runs dry, they know no better than to have it towed back to the shop? What if their vision is failing them? What if their attention to driving and car maintenance is distracted by kids or an elderly parent in the car?

You get the point. I don't mean to minimalize patients' issues, because we who staff the hospital or doctor's office have many more issues to clarify with the patient before they leave the shop/office/hospital than a mechanic does after an auto repair. We need to be very intentional about asking our patients about all the factors that will affect their success (like Social Determinants of Health) when released from our watchful eye. Assess then address.

Certainly, we should schedule their "maintenance" appointment and be in contact with them a few days after their discharge to assess progress. Beyond that, though, we have the responsibility to teach them how to operate their "vehicle." Instruct them on the importance of routine maintenance and on what the dashboard warning lights mean. Figure out ways to help them ensure they have the fuel needed for their journey. Build an appropriate Plan of Care based on a full assessment of the situation and then longitudinally support the person as they learn self-management of their car ... their condition.

When considered in this context, it's obvious we not only need a vast array of assets and services on our potential care management menu, we also need the flexibility to rearrange our typical ingredients into a custom-made recipe designed to support a patient longitudinally through a distinctive set of circumstances and ensure their Home Success Rate.

Home Success Rate?

There may be other terms that might serve better than "Home Success Rate," but I think the time has come for us to reframe the issue of readmissions into a positive, patient-centric measure that encourages us to approach each patient as an individual with unique challenges and issues along their journey in order to optimize their health and well-being. What we call it is not as important as the perspective from which we approach it.

Here I'll throw a monkey wrench into the gears for all of you addicted to the Thirty-Day Readmission Rate: If we improve and encourage the effective self-management of chronic disease, strangely the inpatient admission rate for these conditions will go down and readmission rate will go up. The rationale behind this phenomenon is fairly straightforward. If we decrease the need for admission in mild to moderate severity patients, the severity of those patients admitted will skew toward the sickest and most fragile, and these patients will always have a higher propensity for decompensation and readmission. By eliminating the "easy" admissions, we add bias to our baseline, leading to a higher proportion of (fewer) admissions of sicker patients—resulting in readmissions.

In this case, facilities will need to be monitoring a different metric (like Ambulatory Care Sensitive Condition Admissions—ACSC) to track issues and successes. The percent of ACSC admissions provides a metric to assess how well common chronic conditions are managed in the outpatient world. If the majority of a community's COPD or HF patients are kept out of the hospital, the ACSC admission rate would be low, signaling success–merely a thought as we transition to a different paradigm of care. Just as our motivations and processes need to change, our current and conventional metrics will likely need to be modified as well.

—

CHAPTER SEVEN

Not Two Canoes

IN THE DISCUSSIONS OF Healthcare's move from volume to value, you may have heard many healthcare executives, especially those in health systems, describe their attempt at transition as "a foot in two canoes." They are highlighting the instability associated with transferring from one model of care and reimbursement to another. They feel the need to make a slow and cautious transition, keeping one foot firmly in the volume canoe while gingerly placing the other foot in the value canoe. Sudden or erratic movements might upset both boats and land the executive in the river.

While I understand the metaphoric implications of trying to stand in two separate, unstable watercraft, the description falls short of what's really needed. If the point of the transition were just to move to one canoe from another, all the while paddling the same path on the water, as dictated by the river, one could ask why we need to make the move at all. (And many healthcare executives ask just that question!)

When making the change from a volume-based revenue system to a value-based revenue system, we do have a foot in one canoe: volume. However, the other foot, the value foot, is actually in a helicopter.

We are not stepping from one particular vehicle into an identical vehicle, or even an upgraded version of itself (canoe or any other type of boat), continuing to traverse the same avenue (the winding path of water). In the move to value, we are no longer choosing to get from point A to point B along the meandering path of a river we didn't design and whose path we don't and can't control beyond how and how fast we can paddle. Metaphorically, the move from volume to value takes us out of the water and into the airspace.

The risks, vulnerabilities, and obstacles are different from the river, and we have a bit more control over our path and trajectory around, under, over, or through those hazards. Identifying and learning to navigate through or around these obstacles is the groundwork that an organization needs to lay as it considers the jump to value.

The image of trading one canoe for another one falls short of the true transition to value and, frankly, does not do it justice. The value world is different. The modes of operations are different, and, honestly, this can be frightening to us as we consider taking our feet out of the volume canoe. The hard work of learning, preparing, and planning must consequently be done with discipline. Anything short of that will leave one floating in (not on) the river, hanging on to the gunwale of the destabilized canoe.

As with any transition, however, there is a moment that requires a leap of faith. Uncertainty always presents itself when we eventually let go of one process, principle, or paradigm and shift our weight to the other. Yet if

Here's a secret: Around the riverbend is a waterfall. The current volume model is not sustainable. A change is around the corner, one way or another.

our grasp is firm and our footing sure, we will be more likely to succeed in the jump—and thrive.

This leap is where I've seen health systems fall short in the transition and transformation. By not fully grasping the profound differences between volume and value, many healthcare executives have let the fear of leaving the volume canoe prevent them from making the leap into the value helicopter. This leaves their organization straddling the canoe and the chopper–a dangerous way to pilot a canoe and a terribly inefficient way of flying a helicopter.

By choosing not to embrace fully the change to a mode of practice in which the majority of their revenue comes from value or even choosing to stay in the realm of a volume majority, these executives put their organizations at risk of swamping the canoe. Meanwhile, their hesitancy leaves their value helicopter hovering low and slow, still following the path of the volume river. Maneuvering a rotary-wing aircraft in such an inefficient manner will soon burn all its fuel and not get the pilot to the intended destination.

If we have tried to cushion the blow of the transformation from volume to value by convincing ourselves that it's an easy change to a similar vehicle and that we can continue indefinitely with a foot in both spaces, then we have done ourselves and our patients a great disservice. Here's a secret: Around the riverbend is a waterfall. The current volume model is not sustainable. A change is around the corner, one way or another.

So, don't sell the transition short by simply thinking the process is about moving from one canoe to another. It's about much more than that. By the same token, don't limit the future possibilities in value, thinking you'll still be paddling down the same river albeit in a different canoe. With a true move to value, the sky's the limit.

—

CHAPTER EIGHT

Boiling the Ocean One Bucket at a Time

WE SAY MANY ODD THINGS in business meetings—such as putting lipstick on a pig, moving the needle, having a foot in two canoes, drinking from a firehose, looking under the kimono (WHAT?!)—and yet we always seem to know what's meant. Those of us who deal daily in Population Health initiatives frequently hear euphemisms for wasting time or effort by trying to do too many things at once: trying to solve world peace, trying to boil the ocean, or needing to eat the elephant one bite at a time.

Wait—why are we eating an elephant? Is this the same elephant in the room when I and two blindfolded colleagues all described to the group what we were experiencing to demonstrate the concept of perspective? What did the elephant do to justify its slow but steady consumption? Why the change in our pachyderm affinity?

Even though it deals with dining, I have some real issues with the elephant analogy.

I can get behind world peace, though. It's true that if we first make peace with ourselves, and then with our neighbors, peace will eventually extend across the globe. In healthcare, before we can effectively care for anyone else, we should work toward optimizing our own health and well-being. Then, we will be more effective in our efforts to affect the healthcare of our neighbors positively. This gets a little too personal, warm, and fuzzy for many healthcare execs, though, so they tend to speak of boiling oceans (or eating elephants!).

As regards trying to achieve seemingly impossible goals in our care of patients—sustaining people in their health journeys, addressing their physical, social, emotional, and psychological needs as we support and guide them—how in the world is all that that even possible?

The phrase gets used most often when we're discussing the needs of patients, especially those on the fringes, and how we must rise to meet those needs. During the discussion, a wise and weathered executive will look over the top of their glasses, give a dismissive glance and say, "Well, let's not try to boil the ocean." Honestly, that's great advice. If we can avoid such a colossal task, let's do so.

So, we then separate some patients into a specific cohort to investigate the efficacy of some initiatives that we feel will influence their health and well-being positively. When discussed in the next meeting, someone (oftentimes the same executive as above) will proclaim, "You're separating these people into buckets. It's too confusing. If it's that good, shouldn't we be doing this for everyone?"

Our mission, should we choose to accept it, is the extraordinary task of helping people make their lives healthier.

This happened to me not too long ago, and the light bulb went on in my head. Yes! We are trying to boil the ocean, and yes, we are separating folks into buckets. *We're trying to boil the ocean, one bucket at a time!*

Our mission, should we choose to accept it, is the extraordinary task of helping people make their lives healthier. This is a huge undertaking with multiple variables added to confounding logistic, practical, and process limitations. It looks a lot like boiling the ocean. But if we start with one bucket of water and learn from the process undertaken, we can then apply those lessons to the next bucket and the lessons from that bucket to the next, and so on. Eventually, yes, we will have boiled the ocean.

In healthcare, we like to separate patients into specialized and hyper-segmented disease buckets; diabetes here, COPD/ emphysema there, heart failure over there, etc. This isn't all bad—if we would only apply the lessons learned from each cohort to the others. Typically, though, we keep them isolated in their buckets and start the process from scratch with each disease state within which we try to intervene.

The reality is this: *The Framework of support for these chronic conditions looks very similar if you remove and replace some of the specific names of medications or treatments they receive.*

The goal of effective self-management requires the same supporting structure for each patient; only some of the details are changed. What we sometimes fail to recognize is that the framework of managing care and supporting patients in one bucket extends in similarities to other buckets as well. Many of the needs of a person undergoing joint replacement or heart surgery are the same as one from a chronic disease bucket. We change some details here or there, but the framework for managing their care and leading them to self-management remains pretty much the same.

Oh, but patients from different payer sources aren't sufficiently similar for this model (some say—and they're usually talking about Medicaid or uninsured patients). Or are they? Regardless of who's paying the bill–Medicare, Medicaid, a Managed Care or Commercial plan, or No One–the necessary support and guidance remains basically the same. Social Determinants of Health and the risks associated with those determinants must be considered and addressed in all patients.

True, their specific needs may vary and require a higher concentration of services or resources for one segment. But if, in one group, you can uncover and successfully address issues relating to transportation, food insecurity, childcare, elder care, medication acquisition and adherence, connectivity, interpersonal violence, etc., you can apply the solutions to all the other groups too. Likewise, no one is immune to Behavioral and Mental Health issues and the negative effects those conditions bring with them. Solve that in one bucket, and you can apply those learnings to every other bucket.

If, in one group, you can uncover and successfully address issues relating to transportation, food insecurity, childcare, elder care, medication acquisition and adherence, connectivity, interpersonal violence, etc., you can apply the solutions to all the other groups too.

I now proudly proclaim myself to be an ocean-boiler. I want to find ways to reach all our patients to support them in their journeys to healthier lives and improved well-being. Perhaps you'll see me down at the beach, buckets in hand, scooping out a bucketful and learning how to work with that segment of water, applying the lessons learned to the next, and then the next.

When I've presented this concept to other people, some have quickly jumped to the allegorical story of the person on the beach saving the starfish. I suppose the reference to the beach and going back and forth from the ocean with buckets of water reminds these people of that famous starfish story.

For those unfamiliar, I will paraphrase this parable that's been told numerous times in numerous ways:

> *One morning a person was walking along the beach when, up ahead, they noticed someone picking something up and throwing it into the ocean. Approaching the person, the beach-walker asked, "What are you doing?"*
> *The person replied, "Throwing starfish back into the ocean. The surf is down, and the tide is going out. If I don't throw them back, they'll die."*
>
> *The beach-walker, noticing the beach littered with hundreds, maybe thousands of starfish, exclaimed, "Don't you realize there are miles and miles of beach and hundreds, even thousands of starfish? Surely you can't make a difference!"*
>
> *After listening politely, the person bent down, picked up another starfish, and threw it back into the surf. Then, smiling at the other, said, "I made a difference for that one."*

I first heard this story as a Midwesterner, unfamiliar with the ocean or sea life, and I was truly inspired by the vision, empathy, and determination of the Starfish Thrower. It was only after I moved to the Gulf Coast of Florida that I learned that most starfish (and other shellfish) die from the trauma of being thrown into the water. They can be tenderly lifted, carried to the water, and gently replaced. That works, but…don't throw starfish. It kills them.

This is also a great analogy for how we often deal with the needs and social risks of our patients. We think we know what's best and act accordingly, not realizing that all the while we are actually making things worse.

Population Health is about improving the health of a population, one patient at a time. For the individual, we need to recognize, uncover, and help them deal

We think we know what's best and act accordingly, not realizing that all the while we are actually making things worse.

with the social risks affecting their health and lives. As I noted in the chapter on Social Determinants as vital signs, we will be most effective in addressing a patient's or a population's risks if we engage the patient in shared decision-making, prioritize their various needs, and address them in a way that will benefit the patient, not cause them harm (see Social Needs).

This is why grand, overarching, rigid processes alone are not successful in addressing Population Health, creating value, mitigating Social Risks, or modifying the health of individuals. It's far better to assess our patients for their unique social or other risks so that our Plans of Care can be informed and targeted to their specific and acknowledged needs, not the needs we think they may have or the solutions we think they need. Can we afford to spend all time and resources on the assessment and mitigation of all these needs? The better question is can we afford not to? Social, behavioral, and mental health risks are pressing on our patients from all sides, interfering with our solely medically prescribed plans and preventing the best outcomes for our patients.

So, let's get to work (mindfully). There's a lot of ocean out there to boil, but we can do it, one bucket at a time.

Image by Tourmaline the Whale Productions 2019

Closing Remarks

———

How HAS THE HEALTHCARE industry been able to survive without a primary focus on value creation and attention to its patients? Primarily through the combination of a volume-based, fee-for-service model of service delivery with the reimbursement coming from a third party, not the entity actually receiving the services. This disconnect will continue to lead us down a dysfunctional path of health and well-being in this country. We'd do much better to transition, or better yet, transform intentionally and wholeheartedly, into a healthcare industry that creates value, basing all of our strategies, plans, and actions on a value-based system.

Value-based Care is a better option over Volume-based Care for achieving our ultimate goal in medicine: allow the patient to feel cared for while optimizing their health and well-being.

We've looked at value and its composition and we've explored what it means to focus on value's creation in healthcare. Hopefully, by now you understand the why behind making a shift.

Value-based Care is a better option over Volume-based Care for achieving our ultimate goal in medicine: allow the patient to feel cared for while optimizing their health and well-being. As a system designed around the best interest of healthcare consumers (patients), Value-based Care will allow for the appropriate flow of revenue to the creators of value in the industry.

Value creation depends on maximizing quality and experience while reaching the lowest possible cost. As components of the Value Equation, the three pillars of Population Health and value in healthcare are Risk Stratification (cost), Plan of Care (quality), and Longitudinal Support (experience). Value is relational, volume is transactional. Value is longitudinal, volume is episodic. Value relies on members; volume relies on encounters. A volume paradigm does not even consider quality and experience. Value and Volume are very different, so prepare yourself for the change!

In addition to that major point and perspective, I invite you to consider and act on the following:

1. Population Health Management, the vehicle through which we can deliver value, helps identify the overall, prevalent needs of a specific cohort as well as the risks faced by patients down to the individual level. Those risks are stratified into risk priorities and then used in

directing the care to address solutions. In stratifying the risks, as noted above, we must go beyond the medical diagnoses and conditions to include social risks and needs plus Behavioral/Mental Health risks and conditions. To exclude social and psychological issues greatly limits the efficacy of a Plan of Care as we treat and serve patients.

2. Social Determinants of Health (SDoH) can be positive or negative in their influence on a person. We in healthcare need to assess SDoH in all patients just as we do physical vital signs, so we can identify and address any Social Risks that are negatively affecting their health or well-being. Without this step, and without consideration and attention, the strictly medical prescriptions we provide for a patient's Plan of Care will fall short of our goals and may well fail completely.

3. Beyond Risk Stratification, in order to create value a viable Population Health Model must have a diverse and appropriately staffed menu of care and support options for patients to engage fully and improve the lives of the patients being served. No uniform recipe for success exists across all regions and markets, but if the

concepts mentioned are applied, you will find the best ways of addressing your patients' needs. Having these active processes in place to address various risks and situations in specific patients is much more important than the level of depth or even accuracy found in a risk identification and stratification tool. Risk Stratification without action is merely an academic exercise.

4. Communication and coordination are the lynchpins of Longitudinal Support. Without them, the model falls apart, leaving the patients in the gap to fend for themselves. Value-based Care is a team endeavor, and all the members of the Interdisciplinary Team (IDT) need to be executing the Plan of Care in a high touch, coordinated manner, appropriately applying the right blend of relationship and technology, reaching each individual's specific and unique needs. The patient's complexity, the local resource availability, and the regional expectations will all direct and drive the exact membership on the IDT. Through effective coordination and communication, a patient can feel cared for and empowered by their caregivers.

    Special note: Don't rely on billable services or claims

generation to determine the composition of your IDT. Know ahead of time how much revenue can be generated by being at-risk for the care of a cohort of patients and determine how best to create value with those resources. Spending $100,000 on "non-revenue generating" roles may save you and the patients $1,000,000. When you start with the at-risk revenue in order to achieve net savings rather than starting at zero and trying to generate revenue only through volume, the appropriate application of resources and team members, though not generating a bill, can generate real-money savings to the bottom line by improving the health and well-being of the patients. Again, system and process design that first considers the needs and best interest of the consumer will allow the revenue needed to support the platform.

5. Providers and health systems need to learn from their experiences with one cohort and apply those learnings to as many other groups as possible (my bucket boiling analogy). The basic framework for managing patient care is truly very similar, regardless of the cohort being managed. Without an effective communication and coordination platform that allows for the free flow of

up to date information, you'll likely overcomplicate it through hyper-segmentation and succeed only in confusing or isolating the patient.

6. Don't throw the starfish. Involve patients in the development of their Plan of Care, including the alleviation of Social Risks.

By attending to value in the care we deliver and by valuing the patient and the staff and providers rendering the care as worthy human beings, we can transform health and healthcare in the US to be both more effective and efficient. Improving outcomes (quality) and appropriately lowering costs while supporting our patients and staff is possible through Value-based Care. Application of this model will move the US from its high-spending, poor outcome position in the world to a healthy leader. Can you imagine what could be done with every percentage of our GDP we aren't spending on healthcare if that money were freed up for other purposes?

CPSIA information can be obtained
at www.ICGtesting.com
Printed in the USA
LVHW081359130222
711044LV00015B/110/J